Faeries and Folklore of the British Isles

An illustrated guide to goblins, ghosts, faeries, pixies, mermaids and monsters

Elizabeth Andrews

ARRIS BOOKS
An imprint of Arris Publishing Ltd
Gloucestershire

First published in Great Britain in 2006
by
Arris Books
An imprint of Arris Publishing Ltd
12 Adlestrop, Moreton in Marsh
Gloucestershire GL56 0YN
www.arrisbooks.com

Text and illustrations copyright © Elizabeth Andrews 2006

The moral right of Elizabeth Andrews to be identified as copyright holder of this work has been asserted by her in accordance with the Copyright, Design and Patents Act 1988

ISBN 1-84437-065-8
9781844370658

All rights reserved
A CIP catalogue record for this book is available from the British Library

Printed and bound in China

Telephone: 01608 659328
Visit our website at www.arrisbooks.com or email us at info@arrisbooks.com

CONTENTS

Introduction.......................... 5
Survival Kit........................... 6
Origins................................. 7
Cornwall.............................. 9
Festivals.............................. 21
Devon................................. 22
Somerset............................. 25
Faerie Rings......................... 34
Dorset................................. 36
Changelings........................ 41
Guernsey............................. 42
Sussex................................. 44
Berkshire............................. 46
Faerie Plants........................ 47
Wiltshire.............................. 49
Oxfordshire......................... 51
Buckinghamshire................. 53
Suffolk................................. 54
Faerie Trees......................... 56
Cambridgeshire................... 60
Herefordshire...................... 62
Gnomes............................... 63

CONTENTS

Wales	64
Faerie Islands	73
Shropshire	74
Lincolnshire	76
Derbyshire	77
Cheshire	79
Lancashire	80
Yorkshire	83
Cumbria	88
Durham	91
Northumberland	92
Ireland	94
Isle of Man	104
Faerie Glamour	108
Scotland	110
Elves	129
Other Faerie Sites	138
Check List	140
Additional Reading	143
Index	145

INTRODUCTION

I hope this book will be an invaluable guide for all those people who are still looking for Faeries at the bottom of their gardens.
It is packed with useful information about the different types of Faeries that can be found, and also their customs and habits.
At the beginning of each County is a map indicating the areas where the Faeries are most likely to be found or have been spotted in the past. (Related stories are included.)
Some areas have very little Faerie activity but others like the West Country, Wales, Scotland and Ireland have more than enough for the enthusiast to get stuck into.

Included next to some entries is an X Use caution when approaching these particular beings (in fact don't approach at all!)

Jamjars and nets are useful when catching and examining the smaller varieties but please handle with care as they are easily damaged, and it is most important that they are replaced exactly where they are found.
Always remember that Faeries will pine away and die if kept in captivity.

The best time to see Faeries.
Dawn, Dusk, Midnight, but the crowing of the Cock will drive them away.

The best days are Halloween Oct 31, May Day, Midsummer Day June 24, Lady Day March 25, Christmas Day.

Remember to take some protection against the more unfriendly Faeries.

Rowan is protection against Faerie spells also Ash can be used. Iron repels them and remember they cannot cross running water.

Survival Kit

These are a few things that are essential (in my opinion) for the Faerie spotter to have at hand when attempting to locate certain members of the Faerie tribe.

This book of course!

Horseshoe. Iron repels all Faerie kind and if I'm wrong and it doesn't, a swift blow to the top of their little heads should do it.
A Iron pin is lighter but it doesn't have the obvious advantage of the heavier Horseshoe.

A stout walking stick made of Rowan; this has two uses, one, the Rowan is protection against evil magic and two, again can be used in self defence!

A net is always useful.

Jamjar

Remember to wear stout walking boots as many of the sites listed are not within easy walking distance of roads, pubs etc.

Warm clothing is essential especially a change of socks, underpants etc. Plus remember to pack loads of patience as Faerie spotting requires a lot of sitting about waiting for the little things to show up. That's why you need a change of underpants, wet grass, in case you were wondering. Mind you if you do come across some of the more nasty ones perhaps ....?

Gifts are always welcome by the Faeries, so perhaps taking a small amount of grain, milk, honey would be a good idea. It can be left on the ground for them, I'm sure they will find it.

Signs of Faerie presence.

Even if you cannot see them, you may see unexplained movements of branches or leaves, rippling of water if you are near a lake or stream, a small cloud of dust at your feet, a feeling of chill fingers on your skin, and of course a loss of time. You may see a sudden movement out of the corner of your eye, this can all mean that a Faerie is near.

See also the section on Faerie Plants. This contains some useful tips on enabling you to see them.

Rowan

ORIGINS

There are many explanations as to the origins of faeries but the belief in them is widespread all over the world.

In Norse mythology faeries came from the maggots that crawled from a giant's corpse. Some became light elves that were happy and good, the others became dark elves that were evil and lived below ground.

The Icelandic version is that Eve hid some of her children from God because she was so ashamed that they were dirty. When asked if that was all of her children she foolishly said yes, and so because God knew that she was lying, those dirty children were doomed to live forever in the dark and avoid the sight of man.

Perhaps Faeries are just a small breed of beings who have withdrawn farther and farther into the wilderness to avoid the larger man.
There are other explanations, that they are nature spirits or maybe fallen angels.
Whatever the explanation they come in all shapes and sizes, good and evil, and they survive no matter what this modern generation throw at them and tales of the Faerie folk will still be told long after we are forgotten.

They have populated the British Isles and parts of Europe since the Neolithic and Bronze ages.
They are most common here but small groups of Faeries have been spotted in America.
When the early settlers left for America they unknowingly took with them some small passengers. These early faerie pioneers and their descendants can still be found in the Appalachian Mountains, the Ozarks and other remote areas.
One group even attached themselves to a group of American Indians; the Passamquaddy tribe, who lived near the Canadian border. These faeries were rumoured to be really ugly but luckily only the tribe of Indians could see them, they were supposed to be covered in facial hair and made of stone.

The word fairy comes from the Latin fata or fate.

The old English term for Faerie is fey which means enchanted or bewitched. The state of enchantment is fayerie which gradually changed to faerie and fairy.

'If thou wouldst see Faeries'

Take a pint of sallet oyle and put it in a glasse, first washing it with rose water. Then put thereto the budds of hollyhocke, of marigolde, of young hazle and the tops of wild thyme. Take the grasse of a Faerie throne, then all these put into the glasse........dissolve three days in the sunne, and keep it for thy use.

CORNWALL

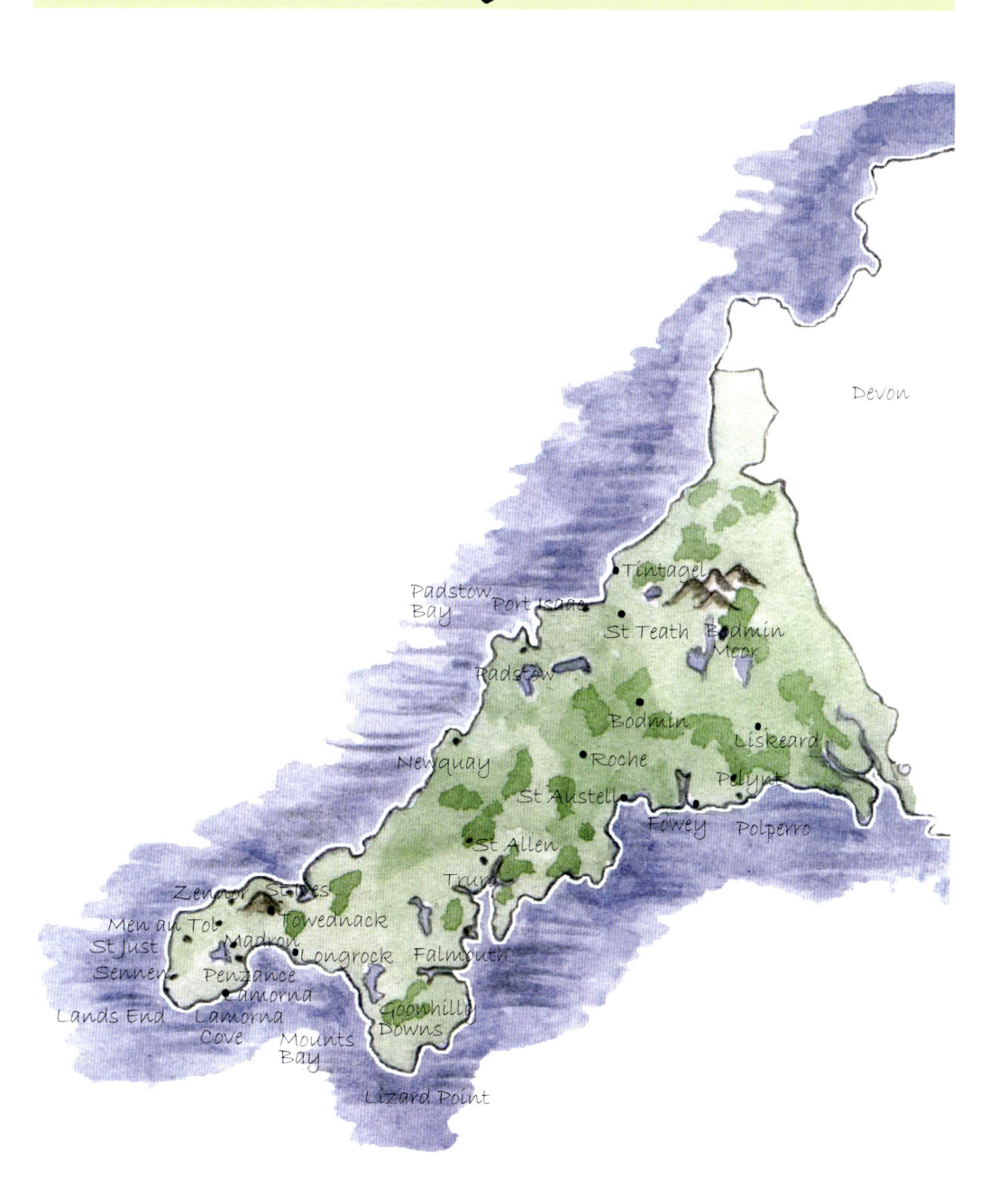

CORNWALL

Cornish Knockers:
Small thin limbed creatures with large hooked noses. They knock with their hammers to indicate a vein of Ore, so gaining their name. Whistling offends them, food or tallow must be left for them or they will be angry. Cousins to the Welsh Coblynau, who also inhabit mines. The Knockers can still be found in some of the abandoned tin mines waiting for the shafts to be reopened.

A miner called Tom Trevarrow refused to share his pasty with the knockers one lunchtime, the next day a rock fall nearly killed him, only his tools were crushed by the rocks.

The Miner suffered from continuous bad luck after that until he was forced to leave the mine for his own safety.

Muryans: Muryan is the Cornish name for ant.
The Cornish believe that Faeries were the souls of ancient heathen people, who were too good for Hell but too bad for Heaven.
So stuck in between they gradually grew smaller and smaller down to the size of ants where they disappeared completely.

The Well at Polperro contains many small Brass Pixies that have been thrown in for good luck. The waters of the well are also used to cure eye problems.

The Old People: another Cornish name for fairies

The Small People of Cornwall.

Gathornes, another name for Cornish mine spirits.

Bwca- a name for a mine spirit Bogie.

Tommy Trevarrow, Tommy Trevarrow,
We'll send thee bad luck tomorrow,
Thou old curmudgeon,
To eat all thy baggan,
And not leave a didjan for Bwca.

A Faerie dwelling can be seen somewhere along the cliffs of Cornwall.
It has been spotted many times by the local fishermen. Hundreds of tiny candles illuminate the terraced gardens of the Faeries.
The sound of music and the scent of the flowers would reach the fishermen in their boats but they would quickly set sail to avoid being enchanted.

CORNWALL

Portunes: Small agricultural faeries, only a half inch high. Small and wrinkled with patched clothes. At night after their labours on the farms they sit around fires and roast frogs to eat. They are England's oldest known faeries.

A hill in Cornwall named the Gump near St Just is a meeting place for Faeries. They are often seen here dancing and feasting. Well mannered observers are welcome and are often given small but precious gifts, but be careful not to offend them.

Tales are told of the Faerie Rade when the King and Queen of the Faeries ride in procession with their followers. All are mounted on white horses hung with silver bells. They are the high born of the Faeries world and spend their time hunting and feasting. They are a common sight all over the country.
Once in Cornwall as they were feasting on the Gump, a faerie hill, an old man from St Just tried to steal their treasure as the faeries sat at their ease. As he stretched out his hand for the gold and jewels, everything became black and he was rooted to the spot. When he came around he was lying on the Gump alone, the faeries, their banquet and treasure had vanished.

CORNWALL

The Cornish equivalent of the Yeth Hounds of Devon are the Devils Dandy Dogs.
This pack is led by the spirit of a priest called Dando, who was spirited away by the Devil for daring to hunt on the Sabbath.
The Priest and his dogs are often heard in full cry as they race across the countryside at night.

A Faerie called Skillywidden was found sleeping under a haystack and was taken home by a Farmer in Zennor, the little Faerie was later rescued by two more faeries who turned out to be his parents.

St. Nun's Well at Pelynt is situated in a grove of Thorn and Oak (both very magical trees).
The water collects in a stone basin and is protected by local Pixies. An offering of food must be left for them if you visit this Well otherwise they will be very offended.

St Teath: There are many tales of people visiting Faerieland and it happened many years ago to a servant girl called Anne Jeffries. She was sitting in her employer's garden doing some mending when she noticed some tiny men coming across the lawn towards her. One of them climbed into her lap, covered her neck with kisses and then gently touched her eyes.
Everything went black and there was a loud rushing noise and when Anne opened her eyes she had been transported to Faerieland. Anne stayed there for many days with her new friends until the tiny men started to squabble over her, she was then taken back to the garden and Anne was surprised to find that she had only been gone a few minutes.
This was the first of many meetings that she had with the Faeries; they passed on many of their healing crafts, unfortunately this then brought a charge of witchcraft against her and she was sent to Bodmin Gaol.
Anne claimed the Faeries fed her during her imprisonment so she took no food from her Gaolers, the faeries continued to feed her until she was released through lack of evidence.

*Faerie Fair and
Faerie Bright
Come and be
my chosen
Sprite*

Buried treasure always has a Hawthorn growing over it to protect it from Pixies.

In the West of England a Faerie path is called a Trod, although animals avoid them, people seeking a cure for Rheumatism will use them.
However it's probably best not to as an encounter with a Faerie procession can be very unlucky.

In 1843 a Penzance newspaper reported the case of a man who had been charged with ill-treating his young child. It had constantly been beaten by him and the rest of the family since birth, and from the age of 16 months had been made to live outside in one of the outbuildings.
The man's excuse was that the child was a changeling and that his real child had been taken by the Faeries, and amazingly enough the case was dismissed against him.

CORNWALL

Mermaids: Half Woman, half Fish.
Mermaid legends are very old and all are remarkably similar. She is usually seen combing her hair while staring out to sea from a rock.
Some legends say that the Mermaid sits alone because she is longing for the soul that she can only attain by marrying a mortal.
Her presence usually indicates a storm, shipwreck or a drowning.
The Mermaid also lulls sailors to sleep with her sweet singing and then carries them away to the depths of the ocean.

The Whooper of Sennen Cove made a whooping sound from inside a thick cloud of mist. It would appear in clear weather over the Cove signifying a severe storm was approaching.
It had the power to stop any fisherman from passing through the cloud of mist to the sea when a storm was imminent.
The Whooper deserted the Cove when two fishermen, determined to get to the fishing grounds, beat their way through the mist with flails. They should have heeded the whooper's warning because neither were seen again!

Falmouth has a resident Sea Monster called Morgawr (Cornish for Sea Monster).
There have been many sightings since 1926 and some photographs were taken by locals and tourists show a huge mass with several humps.
It has also been seen in the River Helford.

Willy Wilcocks Hole (a cavern below Chapel Hill on the western side of the Harbour) in Polperro is haunted by a Fisherman of the same name. He wandered into the maze of tunnels behind the entrance and found his way into Faerieland but when he tried to return he could not find his way out again. His despairing cries can still be heard echoing around the cave as he wanders endlessly looking for the entrance.

Mermaids Rock near Lamorna got its name from a Mermaid that haunts the rocks there.
Her singing foretells shipwrecks in the area. Local fishermen are drawn to the rock by the beauty of her singing but none are ever seen again.

Carved on a 15thCentury bench end in Zennor Church is the mermaid with long flowing hair, with a mirror and comb who fell in love with Mathew Trewella, a local chorister.

CORNWALL

There was once a chorister at Zennor church called Mathew Trewella. He sang so beautifully that the sound attracted the attentions of a mermaid from the sea. She crept into the church while he was singing and became so enamoured of him that she was determined to use all her powers to win him. The Mermaid would wait for him after church and they would walk together back to the beach. One day Mathew did not appear in church and everybody knew that he had followed the mysterious stranger back to the depths of the sea.
On a still night his voice can still be heard coming from under the waves in Pendower Cove singing to his mermaid bride.

CORNWALL

A Cornish fisherman by the name of Lutey once found a mermaid stranded on the shore when he was beach combing.
In return for him helping her back to the water the Mermaid granted him three wishes.
Lutey thought for a while and then decided he would like to wish for something useful, something that would help others.
So he chose to have the power to break spells, the power to control spirits for the good of others and his third wish was that these amazing gifts would be passed down through his family.
The Mermaid granted these wishes so Lutey carried her back to the sea, as he was lowering her into the waves the mermaid wrapped her arm around his neck and started pulling him into the water. Only by flashing his penknife before her could he break the mermaid's hold.
The Mermaid disappeared into the waves and Lutey hoped that would be the last he ever saw of her, but it was not to be. Nine years later, after using his wishes all that time, the Mermaid returned for him and he had no choice but to return with her to the Ocean.
Lutey's descendents carried on being blessed with the gifts that he had wished for, but there was a price to pay, for every nine years a member of the family would be lost at sea.

The sandbank Doom Bar outside Padstow harbour is the result of a curse placed by a mermaid.
She was fired upon by a drunken local when she was bathing in the waters outside the harbour.
The mermaid was understandably miffed!.

The Mermaid's mirror and comb are symbols of fertility and entanglement.

St Patrick's custom of banishing old heathen women by turning them into Mermaids would account for the large number of Mermaids to be found in the Sea.

All Faeriekind are repelled by Iron

CORNWALL

Spriggans: They are very ugly small creatures and can change shape at will and can also inflate themselves to gigantic proportions.
They roam around the countryside in packs terrorizing the neighbourhood. Spriggans are best avoided as they can be very dangerous.
Human babies are also stolen by them and a very ugly Spriggan baby left in return.

Although some tales say that they are the ghosts of giants who guard the treasure that is buried under prehistoric stones, their behaviour is very unghostlike.

Terrytop- Tom Tit Tot,
A type of English Rumpelstiltskin.
A black thing with a long tail, impet or hobgoblin.

Smugglers came ashore at Long Rock and disturbed a group of Spriggans who were dancing and feasting on the sand banks.
Furious at being disturbed in their revels they charged at the smugglers, swelling as they did so until they had reached gigantic proportions. The men only escaped by setting out to sea again.

CORNWALL

A little boy from the parish of St Allen near Truro strayed from his home to pick some wild flowers in a nearby wood. When his Mother called him in for bedtime he had disappeared.

The villagers searched the surrounding countryside for three days but there was no sign of him, until the last evening when they found the little boy asleep in the woods clutching a wilted bunch of flowers.

When he woke up he told his Mother that he had followed a bird that had been singing to him. It led him deep into the wood where he had met some very small people.

The pixies (for that is what they were) took him to a cave that had jewelled crystal pillars and fed him on wild honey, until the little boy had started to feel sleepy so the Pixies sang him to sleep.

When he woke, he was back in the woods with his Mother and the villagers bending over him.

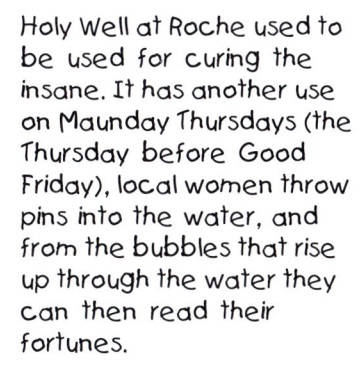

Holy Well at Roche used to be used for curing the insane. It has another use on Maunday Thursdays (the Thursday before Good Friday), local women throw pins into the water, and from the bubbles that rise up through the water they can then read their fortunes.

See Saw Margery Daw,
Sold her bed & lay upon straw,
She sold her straw & lay upon hay,
Piskies came and carried her away.

This little rhyme relates to people being carried away by the little people.

There is a very old belief in the parishes of Morra, Zennor and Towednack that the children of dirty lazy mothers would be taken away by the fairies, carefully washed in the morning dew and then returned, all clean and smelling sweet.

CORNWALL

Madron, Penzance.
The granite Men-an-Tol or Holed Stone lies 2 ½ miles from Madron.
This stone was the entrance to a tomb chamber and the stone itself possesses healing powers. Young children are passed through the hole, naked, nine times; this was believed to cure scrofula, rickets and other illnesses.

Jenny Burnt-Tail, Joan the Wad are the names that the Will o the Wisp is known by in Cornwall.
Jack o Lantern, Joan the Wad
Who tickled the maid and made her mad
Guide me home,
the weathers bad

St Madrons Well is a mile north west of the village. On the first Sunday in May Parents take their ailing children to the well to cure rickets. The child has to be immersed in the water three times while they face the sun, the parents then carry the child nine times around the well.
A strip of the child's clothing is left on a nearby tree as an offering

Faeries are able to appear and disappear at will so to be able to see them try holding a four leaf clover in your hand.

Not all Faeries have wings some can be seen riding Ragwort stalks and flying through the air, others use magic caps or recite spells

Faeries use the down off of Dandelions to travel, so blow on one and help to spread the seed and you will receive a wish in return.

CORNWALL

The Faerie dwelling on Selena Moor near Lands End was first stumbled across about two hundred years ago by a William Nay of Buryan. One night on his way to Baranhaul Farm he became lost in the dark, so decided to take a short cut he knew quite well across the moor. A mist rose and grew thicker and thicker as he struggled on across the marshy ground. Just for a second the bank of mist parted and William could see in the distance some faint lights. By now he was totally lost and in desperation decided to make for the lights, so rode on until he came to a forest that he had never seen before. Hundreds of candles hung from the branches and music drifted about him. The trees became thicker the farther he rode, when at last he came to a small cottage nestled at the base of an enormous tree.

Dancing about a young girl playing a violin, were dozens of little green figures. The sound of the music was so inviting that William felt moved to join in with the dancing until a warning glance from the young girl made him hesitate. She set down the violin and drew him away under a tree, where in the light of an overhanging candle he recognised her as his dead sweetheart Grace Hutchens who used to live in the village of Selena. She had mysteriously died three years before, leaving William broken hearted. The poor girl explained to William that she had become pixy led on the moor the same as William had that night, that she too had been drawn to the cottage by the sound of music and once here had eaten an apple from a tree. From then on Grace was a captive in Faerie land, the body in her grave was nothing but a block of wood woven about with magic to make it resemble her.

William was determined to escape from the Faerie glade and to take Grace with him so he took off one of his gloves, turned it inside out to break the spell and threw it into the middle of the throng. Everything went dark, the Faeries had disappeared, along with Grace, and William fell to the ground in despair. His friends found him there unconscious three days later. William never recovered and shortly after died. His body lies next to Grace in the Buryan graveyard, or does it?.

Menacuddle Well,
St Austell.
This Well is situated in a wood half a mile from the town, people would travel here to cure stomach ulcers by dropping a pin into the waters.

Seahorse: The Greeks called these Hippocampus the sea monster horse. It was supposed to have dark powers, steeped in wine it was used as a poison but the ashes mixed with honeyed vinegar was used as an antidote for other poisons.
It was also thought to cure other illnesses including chills, fevers, baldness and the bite of a mad dog. Chinese apothecaries recommend it as an aphrodisiac.

CORNWALL

Pixies: These are the faeries that live in Somerset, Devon and Cornwall.
They dress in the colours of the earth using materials such as moss, grass and lichen.

They take great pleasure in misleading travellers and also stealing naughty children.

To avoid detection from humans they disguise themselves as hedgehogs.
Local farmers often blame the Pixies if any of their livestock go missing as they have been spotted going for wild rides on the backs of horses, cattle etc

Farmers will leave a bucket of water out at night so that the mother Pixies can wash their babies, and they also leave out a drink of milk as well.
Hearths must be swept every night so that the Pixies have somewhere clean to dance

Moths were believed to be departed souls and are still called pixies in some parts. A green bug which infests bramble bushes in the Autumn are called pixies.

Often places of ancient worship such as stone circles and barrows are avoided as Pixie haunts.

If you step on a Faerie turf it will trigger a mischievous spell, the Traveller will be spun around and end up facing the wrong way.
No amount of trying will he be able to find the right path again. (This is called being Pixy-led.)
To overcome this spell, wear your coat inside out and you should be able to continue safely on your way.

FESTIVALS

These festivals are from the Celtic people who have a deep association with many mystical and magical events, and many of the Faerie beliefs are deeply interwoven with the Celtic way of life.

Imbolc: starts on the 1st Feb and covers Feb, March and April. These celebrations have a strong association with fertility, and are linked with lambing etc. It is also devoted to the Goddess Brigid who was influential in healing and poetry.

Beltane: 1st May. This is a celebration at the start of Summer. It is a fire festival, and bonfires were lit on the tops of hills and sacred sites as part of the celebrations.
In Ireland cattle would be driven between two fires to gain protection against disease.
The eve of Beltane is a magical time when witches and spirits are roaming about the mortal world.
This is also known as Walpurgis Night.

Lughnasadh: 1st Aug. This is a summer festival and marks the final quarter of the Celtic year, and celebrates the gathering in of the harvest. It owes its origins to Lugh, a sun god who has many powers as a magician and warrior.
Lugh later became known as Lughchromain (little stooping Lugh) the forerunner of the Leprechaun.

Samhain: 31st Oct. It is an important fire festival, old fires are extinguished and new ones ceremonially lit from a sacred fire tended by Druids. It marks the beginning of the new year and is also the festival of the dead. This is the time when the souls of the undead return to the world of the living and visit again their old homes. Less friendly spirits also return at this time but can be appeased by offerings.
This was later made All Saints Day by the Christian Church but pagan traditions have survived in the popular celebration of Halloween.

When witches and evil spirits are about on these nights, church bells are rung to stop them from flying over the villages, the villagers would also come out to bang pots and pans and ring hand bells to add to the noise.

During the Beltane Festival Houses and Stables are decked out with branches of Cedar, Sycamore, Hawthorne, Oak, Birch and Fir to encourage fertility.

The central feature of Beltane is the Maypole. Each year a freshly cut tree of Oak, Birch, Elm or Fir is stripped of its branches and decorated with ribbons and flowers, it is then ceremonially burned at the end of the year.

Cattle are singed with Hazel branches at Beltane to keep the Faeries away.

In Ireland and Wales it is traditional on Samhain to sit at a crossroads to listen for the howling of the wind, this will prophesy events for the year to come.

DEVON

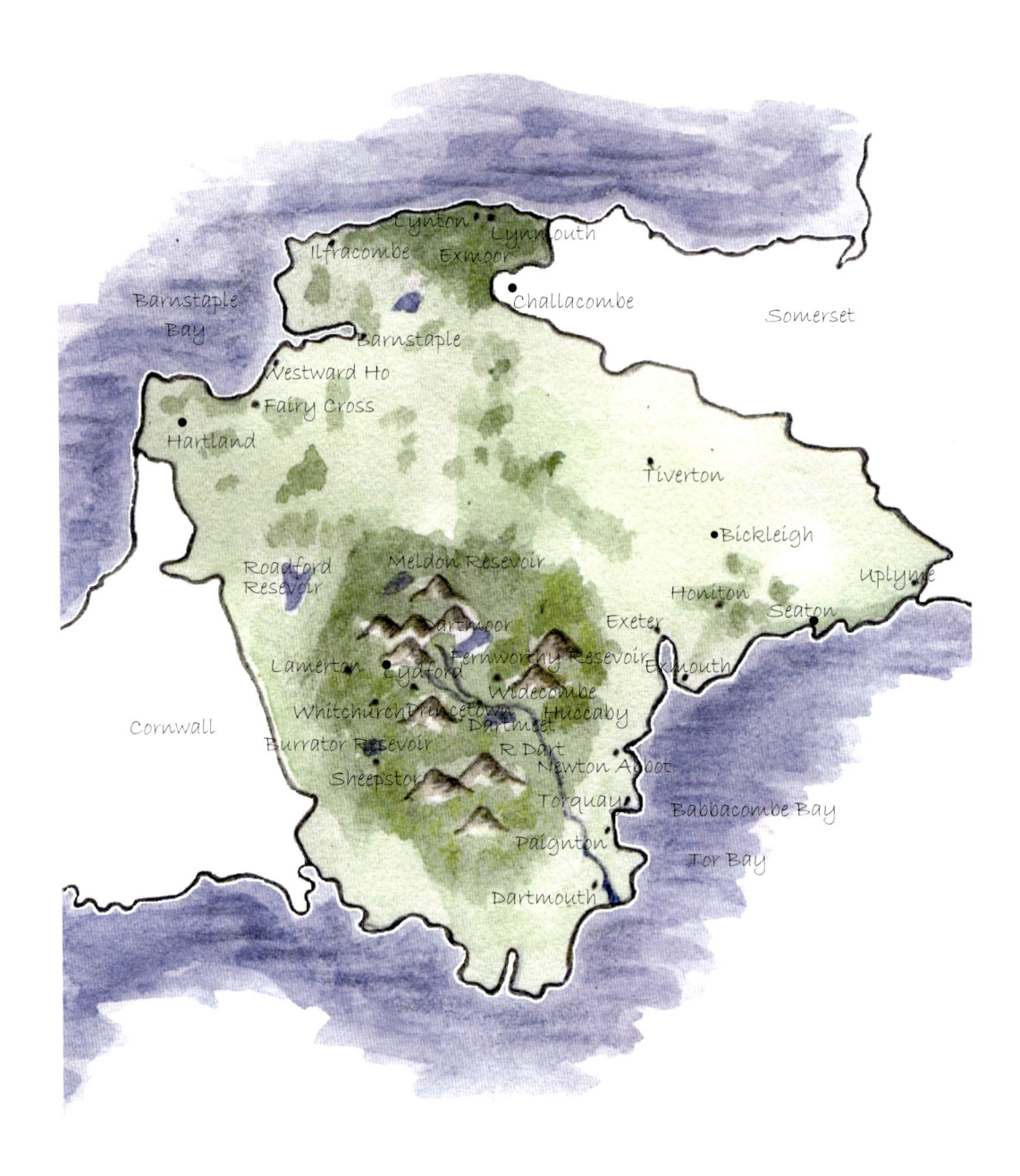

DEVON

Wistmans Wood on Dartmoor is the last remains of an ancient woodland and is the home of a pack of Yeth Hounds. They are a fiercesome sight, jet black, with smoke and flames snorting from their nostrils. From the centre of the woods they start their wild hunt along with a demonic huntsman called Dewer, they race across the wild moorland looking for lost souls. They head for Dewer Stone near Bickleigh where they disappear.
If any mortal is unlucky enough to see them it means banishment to a distant land, and speech with the Huntsman means death.

Heathfield Beacons, Lamerton.
These round Barrows are the scene of a hunt by phantom hounds.

A farm worker's home in Uplyme was plagued by a phantom black dog. Once, losing his temper he took a poker and chased the dog around the house, finally ending in the attic where the Black Dog leapt through the thatched roof.
The farm worker threw the poker after the fleeing dog and where it struck the thatch a stream of gold coins fell from their hiding place. With this money he bought the house on the opposite side of the road and opened an Inn called The Black Dog.
The shadowy form of the black dog can still be seen at times especially in the lane behind the Inn.
The last sighting was in 1959.
(The Inn is now a Guest House)

Broken Barrow, Challacombe.
A treasure seeker disturbed this Barrow in the 17th Century but was driven away before he found anything. The sound of ghostly horsemen terrified him so much that he fled from the Barrow, but as usual he did not escape punishment for disturbing the Barrow. The man was struck blind and died shortly after.

The Harbour at Seaton is constantly silting up due to a Mermaid's curse.
Some local fishermen unwisely insulted her as she was sunning herself off of the coast so she placed the curse in revenge.

Stories of the Yeth Hounds inspired Conan Doyles 'Hound of the Baskervilles'

One well known local legend illustrates the danger of encountering the hounds and huntsman. A local farmer had been visiting the Fair at Widecombe and after spending a few hours in the local tavern decided it was time to set off for home.

Staggering along the lonely road across the Moor he came across the Hounds and Huntsman.

Too drunk to feel afraid he demanded some game from the shadowy figure. With a cold laugh the Huntsman tossed to the man's feet a bulging sack. It was too dark a night to examine the contents, so he swung it to his shoulder and carried it home.

When he got inside he started to open the sack on the kitchen table as he told his wife of his encounter with the dreaded Huntsman.

She was just marvelling on his lucky escape when the dead body of his eldest son fell out of the sack.

DEVON

Whitchurch Down on Dartmoor is a place to be careful as it is still common to become pixie led here.

Near Downhouse, again on the moor, is a pit which Pixies use as a meeting place for dancing and merrymaking.

Pixies Cave, near the village of Sheepstor.
In the jumble of rocks on the village side of the Tor is the entrance to this cave, it is very easy to miss and must be searched for carefully. The short passage leads to a small cave which contains a rough stone seat. There have been Pixies living at this site for many years and they have often been spotted clambering about the rocks near the entrance.

Piskies Holt, Huccaby Cleave, near Dartmeet.
This is a much more substantial dwelling site for the Pixies than the above site, it is a long passage of granite slabs 37 ft long curved with a width of about four feet. At the end of the passage is a small exit hole. This can be found on the left bank of the river amongst the undergrowth.

New Bridge on the River Dart.
The ground between the bridge and the hill is used by the local Pixies for their dances on moonlit nights.

Greywethers, Lydford.
The stones of this ancient circle revolve slowly at certain times of the year when the early morning rays of the sun strike them.

Vixen Tor, Dartmoor
This used to be haunted by an evil witch, who was responsible for many travellers losing their way in the thick mist she would conjure up. The travellers would fall into the bogs of the moor and perish. The witch was disposed of by a local man who obtained a magic ring from the Pixies of the moor. The ring made him invisible so he was able to creep up behind the witch and push her to her death from the top of the Tor.

Hartlands Stone, Hartland turns away from the sound when the nearby church bells begin to toll.

Anybody who laughs long and hard is said to laugh like a pisky, as liking to laugh is a characteristic of Pixies.

Beneath the Faerie rings where the Pixies dance at night gold can be found if you dig deep enough.
Put your ear to the sides of Tors and you will hear the Pixies knocking deep within the rock, or if you are really lucky you will be able to hear the bells being rung in their underground villages.

A poor thresher and his wife once made a little suit of clothes for a Pixie that had been helping them with the threshing. The naked Pixie had crept into the barn every night and steadily threshed while singing to himself,
"Little pixy fair and slim, without a rag to cover him"
The couple had been so grateful for all his help that the wife had cut up one of her own skirts to make the suit for him, she then laid it out in the barn where he could find it that night. The Pixie fell on the clothes with glee singing
"Pixie fine Pixie gay,
Pixy now must fly away"
The Pixie disappeared out of the Barn and that was the last they ever saw of their helper.

SOMERSET

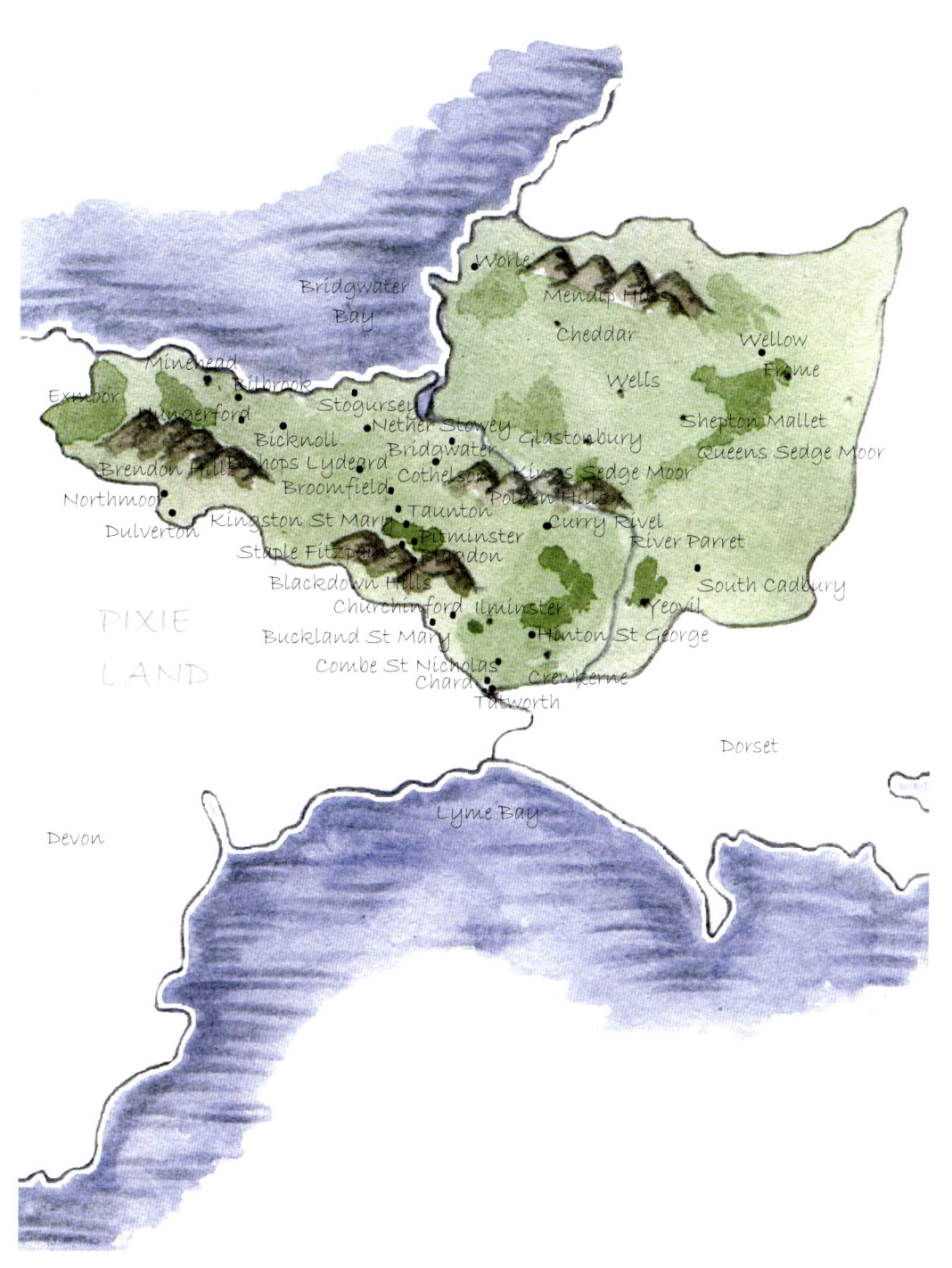

Worle
Bridgwater Bay
Mendip Hills
Cheddar
Wellow
Wells
Frome
Minehead
Kilbrook
Exmoor
Hungerford
Stogursey
Shepton Mallet
Bicknoll
Nether Stowey
Glastonbury
Queens Sedge Moor
Brendon Hills
Bishops Lydeard
Bridgwater
Broomfield
Cothelstone
Kings Sedge Moor
Northmoor
Kingston St Mary
Polden Hills
Dulverton
Taunton
Curry Rivel
River Parret
Staple Fitzpaine
Pitminster
Blagdon
South Cadbury
Blackdown Hills
Churchinford
Ilminster
Yeovil
Buckland St Mary
Hinton St George
Combe St Nicholas
Chard
Crewkerne
Tatworth

PIXIE LAND

Dorset
Devon
Lyme Bay

Somerset

Oak Men: Tree spirits which can be found all over the country. Maybe the trees are the spirits or perhaps the Oakmen are forest Dwarfs who look after the animals of the woods. They can be dangerous if their trees are harmed.
In Somerset angry Oakmen haunt the coppices which spring up around felled Oaks and locals avoid such spots when the sun goes down.

Wick Barrow, Stogursey, is a burial mound that is a known Pixies haunt.
Once a ploughman working in the fields nearby heard a small voice crying in the bushes on the mound. It was complaining that it had broken its peel (a type of flat wooden shovel used for putting loaves into a baking oven).
When the ploughman went to look all he found was a tiny wooden peel with a broken handle. Thinking that a child was hiding in the bushes, he mended it and left it for when the child ventured out.
When he had finished ploughing he returned to see if the child had found its broken peel, it was gone but in its place was a beautiful cake. Still hot from the pixies oven, left as a thank you for the ploughman.

Many years ago Farmers fattened their cattle here, where the pastures were so rich they called it the Summer Land.
Eventually it became known as Somerset.

Buckland St Mary is the last place where the red clothed faeries were seen in Somerset.
They were defeated in battle by the Pixies so now everywhere west of the River Parret is now Pixieland. The Faeries fled to Ireland although a few settled in Devon and Dorset.

SOMERSET

The Holman Clavel Inn near Blagdon has a hearth spirit called Chimbley Charlie.
He sits on the beam above the fireplace. It is best not to offend him as he has a way of making visitors feel very unwelcome.
Their drinks will disappear, the glasses cleaned and packed away, and the table reset for the next guest!

A Great Worm whose girth was larger than three Oak Trees settled in Sherrage Wood near Stogursey.
It ate much of the local livestock and some of the locals as well when they were foolish enough to venture into the wood to gather bilberries.
One old Crone persuaded a Woodcutter from Stogumber to enter the wood and pick some of the berries for her. She conveniently forgot to mention the Great Worm to him!
The Wood cutter gathered a basket full for the Old Woman and then sat down to rest on a log while he had a drink of the local cider.
The log began to move beneath him so he leapt to his feet and chopped it in two with his axe.
One end of the Giant Worm crawled off to Kingston St Mary, the other to Bilbrook near Minehead.
As the two ends never met up again the Giant Worm died.

Somerset

Ruborough Camp, Broomfield.
This Hill Fort is located in the Money field, so called because of the amount of old coins that have been found there.
Within the earthworks lies a Castle of Iron in which a great treasure is guarded by spirits.
To find this hidden treasure the hardy soul has to excavate at noon and in complete silence.

Blackdown Hills:
A playful hobgoblin called Blue Burches lived with a cobbler and his family in the Blackdown Hills. Although it played many tricks on the family, they were horrified when a minister overhearing the Cobbler talking of their hobgoblin, exorcised him! Blue Burches was never seen again.

Cow Castle, Exmoor:
This Hill fort was built by the Faeries to defend themselves against the stronger earth spirits that are much in evidence on the Moors.

Castle Neroche:
In 1854 men eager to find buried treasure started digging at this site. While they were busy with their shovels a mysterious storm blew up out of nowhere, and strange noises came from the ground beneath their feet. The final straw came when they started to hear ghostly voices whispering in their ears. The men fled from the site terrified, but they did not leave soon enough, for within one month each of the men had been struck down by a mysterious illness and all eventually died.

Churchingford, Otterford:
Faerie peddlers hold their markets here, close to Robin Hoods Butts. Mortals who stumble across them are unlucky enough to be struck down with a Faerie paralysis.

A Somerset old Wives Tale is that you should never dress your baby in green until after the Christening as green is the Faerie's colour, and it would enable them to steal the baby away

Faeries hate salt, so good mothers carry salt in their pockets until their baby is christened.

The Will o the Wisp is called Hunky Punk on the Somerset and Devon Border.

The Devil's Whispering Well at Bishops Lydeard can be found behind the Churchyard. This is a 'cursing well', where people would throw offerings into the water along with a curse aimed at a certain person.
The recipient of it would have to visit the well and throw in a more valuable offering to remove the curse.

SOMERSET

Cadbury Castle, South Cadbury:
This Hill Fort was once used by Faeries to store the grain that they gathered from the surrounding plain. The Faeries were driven away by the sound of the newly erected Church Bells nearby. They left so quickly that they didn't even remove the gold from the hidden passageways beneath the mound.
The Faerie treasure can not be found by mortals for the harder you dig for it the farther it will sink into the earth of Cadbury Hill.

The Woman of the Mist is like the Scottish Faerie Blue Hag, who also tends the herds of deer. She is found on Bicknolle Hill and on Staple Plain usually in the form of a frail old crone or sometimes as a great misty figure.

The White Lady of Wellow has a dual function she is the Banshee to the Lords of Hungerford and is also the Well spirit of St Julians.
The sight of her was not welcome however, as it would mean that a disaster would be about to befall the Hungerford family.

In the Quantocks it is a common belief that if you stand beneath an Alder tree on Midsummer Eve you will see Faeries and be granted a wish. But there is a price to pay, you will die within the year.

Sand Martins are Faerie birds, they build their nests in the banks where the Faeries live and are protected by them.

Hammers Walk, Taunton:
A green haired water spirit haunts the stream edge here, the locals call her Spunky.

Griggs; the name for the small red hatted west country Faeries.

Somerset

A faerie market takes place in Pitminster every week; they mingle with the mortals although they cannot be seen by them. The Faeries have the unfortunate habit of stealing money from the Farmers pockets and replacing it with their own.
The Faerie's money will vanish as soon as the Farmer tries to spend it.

An account of a fair, between Pitminster and Chesterford on the Blackdown Hills, was given by a man who came across the fair one day when he was riding back to his home at Combe St Nicholas near Chard.
On the side of the hill was gathered a large crowd of small people dressed in red, green and blue wearing high crowned hats. It looked like a fair to the man, he could see peddlers with trays of trinkets and ribbons mingling with the crowds and set up around the field were tents piled high with various goods.
As he drew nearer to the figures they began to fade and the people nearest to him, he couldn't see at all. But as he passed through the invisible throng he felt himself being pushed and pinched, and when he left the fairground the little figures came back into view. The man decided to leave for home quickly as he was beginning to feel immense pain where he had been touched by the invisible hands. By the time he arrived home a strange paralysis had afflicted him down one side and this continued for the rest of his life.
This particular market has been seen many times since then but nobody ventures too close as the Faeries do not welcome guests to this event.

At Hinton St George the Punky night celebrations on the last Thursday in October is closely linked with Samhain. The children of the village go around collecting candles which are then placed inside scooped out Mangel Wurzels, these 'punkies' are carved with faces, trees or houses. These are carried around the village while a traditional punkie song is sung.
(Turnips and Swedes have been used as well in recent years due to the shortage of mangel wurzels)

The Apple Tree Man is the guardian spirit of Somerset Orchards; he can be found in the oldest tree, also keeping him company is the faerie horse, the Colt Pixy. Also frequenting orchards is Lazy Lawrence. (see p. 39)

The last apples of the harvest must be left for the Pixies. The Somerset names for taking these are Pisking, Col-pixying, Griggling, Pixyhunting and Pixywarding.

The Pixies are very powerful in May so it is best not to wear the colour green during the month as it is their colour; if you do, protect yourself with primroses or forget-me-nots.

The Fisherman of Worle, before setting out to Sea, place a white stone on the Faerie mound and say:
"Ina pic winna
send me a good dinner"
This will ensure that they will have a good catch and return safely.

At Stoke Pero Church the Spunkies come from all around the County to guide the dead of the past year to their funeral service which is held on Halloween, and on Midsummer Eve they return again to greet the recently deceased.

Somerset

Nether Stowey Blind Well is a Faerie Well, these waters have healing powers for the sick.

Dulverton also has a Well with healing powers, these waters cure sore eyes. If you do use the well remember to leave a red rag tied to a bush as an offering to the Guardian of the Well.

Skimmington Well, Rockhill, Curry Rivel:
The waters of this well cure rheumatism, the sufferer must bath in the waters at sunrise for three consecutive mornings to be cured.
People have danced around this Well on Midsummer Day for many years to cure their illnesses.

St Agnes Well, Cothelsone:
This is a Pixies Well and you must leave a pin as an offering if you visit this site.

In this County the Raven is treated with a great deal of respect as bad luck will follow if you attempt to injure this bird. A Farmer called Loscombe who lived at Northmoor Green found this out one day, after taking a shot at a pair of Ravens whilst out riding his fields one day. The two birds were Faeries in disguise and in a fury made the Farmer ride a race all night long around the County borders. He was found the next morning laying in the mud of his farmyard absolutely exhausted.
The farmer did not recover and slowly grew thinner and thinner in his bed until in desperation his wife called in a wise woman from Bridgwater. In exchange for a good meal the woman visited the farm and charmed the evil spirits away. From then on the Farmer thrived but left his gun at home when he rode about his farm.

Pins that cross as they settle in the water of a well after being left are unlucky, if they lie together it foretells a happy marriage and if they drift apart then so will you and your partner.

A coin lying flat after being thrown in to the well is also lucky, but coins must never be removed from a Well as it is very unlucky.
Also your wishes must be made in silence.

In Somerset a faerie ring is called a gallitrap, it is made by the Pixies riding stolen colts round and round a field.

Somerset

Glastonbury Tor:

Glastonbury is a place that is oozing in spiritual and mystical forces, it is the Isle of Avalon, the Faerie Island where the dying Arthur was taken.

Many years ago it was an actual island in the midst of the marshes of Somerset until the drainage programme initiated by the Abbots in the 13th Century.
The Tor is topped by St.Michaels Tower, this particular Saint protects sacred sites by standing to the North of the building.

At the base of the hill is the Chalice Well, this is where the Holy Grail was hidden by Joseph of Arimathea and then found by the Knights of the Round Table. The water from this well has special healing powers and is drunk by the hundreds of pilgrims to this magical site.
There are two further wells, one to the north west of the Tor, the Elder Well (also called St.Edmunds Well) which used to be surrounded by a sacred grove of trees, and nearby to that again, Ashwell Spring.

It was called the Island of Glass.

Avalon in ancient Welsh is Ynyswytryn which means grassy island, in Saxon, Glastney.

The Tor has traces of an ancient maze pathway worked into the side of the hill.

The body of King Arthur was found here, placed with the body was a lead cross on which was engraved in Latin
"Here lies the famous King Arthur buried in the Isle of Avalon"

Arthur was reburied in the Abbey and although it was destroyed by Henry the Eighth his tomb has become a famous Shrine.

Joseph of Arimathea stuck his staff into the ground on the top of Weary All Hill, the staff took root and grew. The Glastonbury Thorn still thrives despite attempts by the Puritans to destroy it. It blooms every Christmas and a sprig is sent to the reigning Monarch each year for the festive table.

SOMERSET

The entrance to Annwyn, Faerieland on Glastonbury Tor is guarded by Gwynn-ap Nudd, The White One, the Faerie King.
His Crystal Realm is the meeting place for the Dead and from the Tor he leads the Wild Hunt on Samhain, on stormy nights he is accompanied by the White Hounds of the Otherworld

Ynnis Witryn, the Crystal Isle

Around the 1400s a Welsh Saint called Collen built himself a hermit hut on the lower slopes of the Tor.
The saint wished to meditate in peace and at that time the Tor was still an Island surrounded by marshland so it was an ideal retreat for him, or so he thought, he didn't realise that the Tor was already occupied by Gwynn-ap Nudd and his court.
One day he overheard two locals talking about the Faerie King and was furious with them that they could still believe in such old superstitions. The two men warned him to be careful of what he said of the Faerie King, as his wrath could be terrible.
Collen refused to listen to their warnings and returned to his meditations. The next day a Faerie messenger appeared at his hut inviting him to a meeting with Gwynn-ap Nudd at the top of the Tor. The same messenger returned day after day until Collen finally agreed to meet with the Faerie King. But before following the messenger to the top, he slipped a flask of holy water inside his cloak. As he reached the top, the familiar landscape of the Tor disappeared and there were the Faerie halls of Gwynn-ap Nudd gleaming with sparkling lights and filled with beautiful music. The Faerie King himself was seated on a golden throne at the end of a vast hall surrounded by his courtiers.
He welcomed the Welsh saint warmly, offering him a drink from a beautiful golden cup, but Collen knew enough of the Faerie ways to refuse the drink. He took the flask of holy water from his cloak and with a sweeping gesture threw the water over the company of Faeries.
Gwynn-ap Nudd, his Faerie palace and courtiers all disappeared leaving Collen alone on the top of the windswept Tor.

But the Faerie King did not disappear forever. He is such a powerful figure that he still remains at the Tor, guarding the entrance to Annwyn.

The Tor has been the scene of some very mysterious light shows, flickering over the hill. In 1981 a strange writhing light was seen arching from the tower and earthing itself near the Chalice Well.

The Dead are sometimes said to have been captured by the Faeries and have been seen in Faerieland

FAERIE RINGS

Faerie rings:- Ring of fungus which grows in grass or turf.
This is where Faeries and Witches gather to dance and sing so it can be a very dangerous place to step in unaware.
If you are drawn inside you can only escape the dancing Faeries if a human chain pulls you out of the ring. You will lose all sense of time and what might have seemed like minutes could have been hours.
But this is the down side of faerie rings, there are some advantages.
If you run around a faerie ring nine times under a full moon this will enable you to see and hear the Faeries, but do not do it on All Hallows Eve or May Eve as these are very important faerie festivals. They would be very offended and carry you off to faerie land.
If you would like a wish granted you have to stand in the middle of the ring under a full moon and it will come true. How you are supposed to do this without getting caught up in the dancing I don't know, but give it a go, just remember to take back-up just in case!.

FAERIE RINGS

There are many mushrooms that form Faerie Rings, some are edible but there are quite a few that are extremely dangerous to eat.
Mostly found in grass but can also be seen in woodland.
Faerie courts, Faerie dances, Faerie walks, and Hag tracks are just a few of the names these rings have been known as over the years.
Some of the Faerie Rings can grow for many years and reach enormous sizes, the largest was supposed to have been 650 metres across and it was believed to be over 700 years old.

St Georges Mushroom.
This one forms one of the largest Faerie Rings, found in fields on chalky soil.

Fairy Ring Champignon.
One of the most common, forms large rings especially on lawns. Appears in early summer after rain.
In Victorian times it was known as Scotch Bonnet.

Cream Clot.
Appears later in the Summer but often grows in the same Ring as the above.

Meadow Puffball.
This is found in grassland including lawns.

Buff Meadow Cap.
Found in grasslands sometimes in open woodlands.

Young girls would often bathe their face in early morning dew to improve their looks, but the dew from inside a Faerie Ring would have the opposite effect. Their skin would erupt in warts and spots.

DORSET

DORSET

Bincombe Hill and Bincombe Down: These hillocks are known locally as the Music Barrows and are occupied by Faeries. If you lay on the top of one at Noon with your ear pressed to the ground, you will be able to hear the faint sounds of a Faerie orchestra.
Another Music Barrow can be found at Whitchurch where midday singing is heard at the top of the mound.

In 1566 John Walsh of Netherbury, who had been accused of Witchcraft, admitted that his powers had come from the Faeries.
He said that they lived in the huge green mounds all over the County and could be asked for advice for one hour at midnight and at noon.
According to Walsh there are three different types of Faeries, green, white and black, the last is apparently the worst.

A mermaid once came ashore on Portland at Church Ope Cove. She was spotted by locals who were on their way to the local Church of St Andrews. The Mermaid was carried into the Church and promptly died.

Cave Hole on Portland is the haunt of a Black Dog called the Roy Dog / Row Dog. During bad storms it lies in wait for the unwary traveller and then pounces on it's victims. The remains are found several days later floating off the coast. It is considered to be a portent of Death if you meet him.

Grange Hill, Creech near Tyneham.
A vast spectral Army marches across the hills from Flowers Barrow to Grange Hill. It is seen mostly at times of national crisis, when the noise of marching feet and clashing of the armour can be heard for miles.
They have also been seen at Knowle Hill.

A Mermaid has often been seen sunning herself on Table Rock off Old Harry Point at Swanage.

DORSET

Veasta: Large sea creature, part seahorse, part fish. This has been spotted swimming off Chesil Beach near Portland. The first documented report was in 1457, it was seen again by the historian Rev John Hutchens in 1757, and was seen again in Church Ope Cove on Portland in 1965.
It is believed that it is not the same creature that has appeared over the last 500 years as the remains of one was washed up on Burton Bradstock beach just a few miles down the coast, and it was believed to be by the locals at the time to be the Veasta.

Many Faeries used to live on the Isle of Portland until the first bells were hung in the Church. At the first peal they left hurriedly along Chesil Beach.

Belemnites, bullet shaped fossils that are found on the beach are called Colepexies fingers.

Stourpaine Church, Blandford Forum.
The Faeries here actually like the sound of the Church bells so much that they creep up into the Belfry before the sun rises each morning to peal the bells themselves.
If you visit the church early in the morning you may be lucky enough to see tiny wet footprints on the stone stairs where they have trodden in the early morning dew.

Fontmell Magna.
There used to be a Barrow at Washers Pit until it was levelled in 1840 to make way for a road, the Faeries that lived in the mound left and moved to the village pond at Ashmore.

Stones with holes in them (p.123) are known as Hag stones, Holy stones, or Faerie Stones in Dorset, as they are considered to be lucky. Fishermen hang them from their boats to bring them a good catch and to ensure their safe return. They are also hung on buildings to ward off evil spirits.
Hag stones placed around horses' necks at night will ensure that they are not stolen during the night by witches or pixies.

Gabbygammies: A name for the noisy chattering Faeries of Dorset.

DORSET

Dorset and Somerset has its own Kelpie called the Colepexy, this, like its Scottish cousin, will take people for a wild ride before dunking them in streams. Also common to both Counties is Lazy Lawrence a wild horse that guards Orchards, it is possible to see him as he gallops through the apple trees but be careful he does not see you as one glance of his green eyes will freeze you to the spot, especially if he thinks you are stealing apples, and there you will stay until sunrise the next morning.

"Lazy Lawrence, let me go
Don't hold me summer and winter too."

This west country ditty relates to the horse's powers over apple stealing humans.

The River Frome especially around Wool is known to be the home of water nymphs, although beautiful they are treacherous and very dangerous.
The Monks of Bindon Abbey (this was destroyed by Henry V111 during the dissolution) knew of their existence and warned one of the local men of the dangers. The man had met one of these water nymphs while walking by the side of the river and had fallen in love with her.
He was horrified when the monks told him that the nymph had no soul and could only survive by drawing life from its victims. Not wanting to believe the monks he rushed to the river bank to find her. Perhaps the Water Nymph had sensed that the Monks had warned him, and although he walked the banks from Wool bridge to Moreton Ford every day he never saw her again.
As the time went on he became more and more heartbroken and eventually threw himself into the water and drowned.

A small troupe of white robed Faeries known locally as Nanny Diamonds can be found around the village of Cheyne. They dislike being disturbed by strangers and have been known to lie in wait and throw stones at travellers walking along the lanes around the village.

The waters of the well at Upwey have healing powers especially for sore eyes.
Take a few sips of water then throw the rest over your shoulder and make a wish.

St Augustines Well, Cerne Abbas:
New born babies used to be dipped into the waters of the well.
And at Easter the faces of people about to die can be seen in the water.

St Candidas Well, Stanton St Gabriel:
Visit it at daybreak if you wish to make use of its healing powers, very effective for sore eyes. Bent pins were thrown in as offerings along with the chant of
'Holy Well, Holy Well,
Take my gift and cast a spell.'

DORSET

Maiden Castle is one of the most famous ancient Hill forts in Dorset, and its Faerie inhabitants live in the mounds found at the ends of the defensive ditches.

The Church of St James at Lecombe was moved from its intended position at East Chelborough by the Faeries of Castle Hill.
It was moved in one night by the little folk, they obviously thought the view was better there!

During certain phases of the Moon a ghostly horde of Faeries, Demons and Witches hunt across Eggardon Hill at Powerstock. They scour the ancient Hill fort looking for the souls of the long dead.
Their eerie cries can be heard across the hill and anybody who ventures out when the hunt is abroad is in certain peril.

Garlic: This has been used for hundreds of years as protection against evil spirits.
Garlands of Garlic worn or hung about the house will help to ward them off and to protect the inhabitants from spells.

Garters: These are, strangely enough, very prominent in folklore and magic as they are potent magical symbols.
They were worn on many pagan rituals, even today morris dancers still wear them.
The colour of the Garter is very significant, green is the colour of Faeries, red is for protection against bewitchment and silver is associated with the phases of the moon.

CHANGELINGS

Faeries will not hesitate to steal un-baptized children, especially popular are fair haired babies, replacing them with changelings.
These may be either an old wrinkled elf who wants an easy life or a replica made of wood which under a Faerie spell will appear to be alive.
The replica will sometimes appear to sicken and die, it would then be buried.
It may continue to live, but it will not grow however much it eats, and changelings do have an inexhaustible appetite, it will also have a wizened deformed appearance.

In earlier years many babies that were born ugly or malformed were believed to be these changelings, as this was an easier explanation for parents of a socially unacceptable child; life would have been hard for these children.
Placing the changeling on a red hot poker or putting it on the fire, or whipping it was believed to make it reveal its true nature. It would then fly cackling up the chimney and disappear, the real baby would be found at the door having just been returned by the Faeries (see page 12).

Offerings of milk were left at the Well of the Spotted Rock, Inverness, by Mothers who believed that their child had been taken by the Faeries and replaced by a changeling. The changeling would then be left overnight near the well and when the Mother returned in the morning, she hoped the real child would be there, having been returned by the Faeries.

Men and Women were also taken to be husbands and wives of Faeries in the otherworld.
In 1894 in Clanmel, County Tipperary, Bridget Cleary fell under suspicion of being a changeling by her husband Michael.
She apparently appeared more refined than usual and had grown an extra two inches.
Although she protested her innocence he tortured and burned her to death "to make the witch confess".
Michael Cleary buried the remains of his wife but they were later discovered and he was charged with manslaughter.
He was sentenced to 20 years hard labour.

Faerie births are becoming rarer and the Faerie children are not as healthy as they once were.
So mortal babies are taken to replenish their stock

The stealing of children has a more sinister motive in the Lowlands of Scotland. Mortal babies are used by the Faeries to pay the Devil's Tithe which is due every seven years.

To protect a baby from being taken by the Faeries hang an open pair of scissors over the cot or stick an iron pin into the baby's clothes.

Lay the Father's trousers across the cot.

Draw a circle of fire around the cot.

Make the sign of the cross above the baby and sprinkle it and the cot with Holy Water.

GUERNSEY

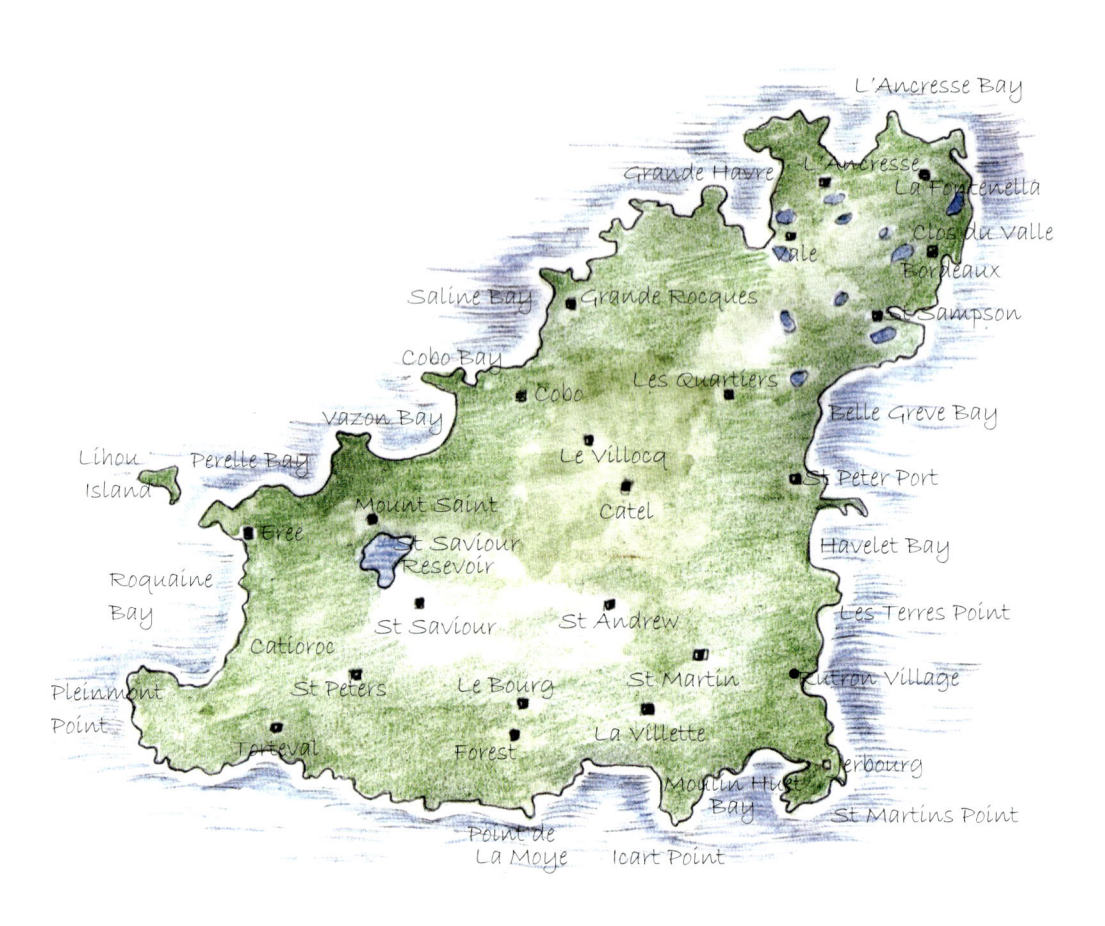

GUERNSEY

On the Island of Guernsey there is a story that is still told of a beautiful young girl called Michelle, who lived on the Island many years ago. She fell in love with a handsome young man that she found sleeping in some leaves under a hedge near her home.

By his size Michelle knew that he was a Faerie but that did not deter her. They were determined to get married, although both sides were not pleased with the match, the families decided they could not stand in the way of true love. So Michelle and her small Faerie sweetheart were married and sailed off together to his Faerie home.

Some time later a local man met a group of small people near Vazan Bay, they had come to get beautiful wives like Michelle.

When the Islanders refused to hand over any more of their young daughters there was a bloody battle which the Faeries won.

So the Faeries had won their Brides but they did not stay long with them and soon returned back to their Faerie home.

And it is said that this is the reason why most of the Guernsey people are small.

Tall Islanders are descended from the only two mortal survivors from that battle.

An ancient burial chamber at St Peter in the Wood is known locally as the Faeries Hole.

The Faeries come out from the cave on moonlit nights and dance on the Catioroc.

A black dog with clanking chains and huge eyes Haunts St Peter Port. Its name is Tchi-co and to hear its howls is a sure sign of death

The appearance of the Dog of Bouley on Jersey means a storm is imminent.

A black dog guards Hidden Faerie treasure at Petit Port.

At Handois in the quarries at the centre of the Island of Jersey you may hear the tinkling of tiny silver bells from a Faerie bridal party.

Sussex

Sussex

There was a Sussex Farmer called James Meppom who owned a small farm in a very lonely spot in the countryside.
His barn stood some way off from his farmhouse so each evening he would trudge back down the track for his supper in the house.
One particular evening after a long day threshing, he closed the barn door and left the pile of threshed corn on the floor to go home for his supper.
The next morning to his surprise the pile of corn was much larger than when he had left it. This went on for several days, until James, being a bold fellow, was determined to see what was happening in his barn every night.
So the next night he hid amongst the straw and waited. Just as he was beginning to doze, for it was getting late and he had been working hard in the fields since early morning, he was roused by the steady thump of some flails. James peeped out from where he was hiding, and there steadily threshing the corn were two little figures no more than eighteen inches high.
When James Meppom saw the two little figures he started laughing and shouted to them asking what they were doing in his barn. The two startled figures rushed for the barn door carrying their tiny flails and as they passed James, clouted him about the side of the head. It was such a savage blow that it laid the poor man out until the next morning.
James struggled home and his Wife, seeing what a state he was in, sent for the Doctor.
Although the Doctor considered it to be just a slight fit James would have none of it and told the good Doctor that he had the curse of the Pharisees upon him. As far as James was concerned he was doomed and strangely enough within the year he was dead.

There are many packs of ghostly hounds that haunt Britain's hills and moors. There is a legend in Sussex that one such pack has its kennels on Ditchling Beacon.
It is unlucky to meet one of these packs as it always precedes a death.

Farisees or Pharisees:
The Sussex / Suffolk name for faeries. Children used to be confused between the farisees and the biblical mention of the Pharisees.

Feriers or Ferishers:
another Suffolk name for Faeries.

Cissbury Ring, Findon:
This hill fort is honeycombed with passages in which lives a huge snake, this has lived here for hundreds of years guarding the vast treasure trove that lies beneath the fort.

Chanctonbury Ring, Washington:
If you run around this hill fort seven times the evil spirits that live here will appear from the grove of trees that grow from the centre of the hill.

Harrow Hill:
These old flint mines used to be home to Faeries but they left the site some years ago when it was opened for an excavation.

Berkshire

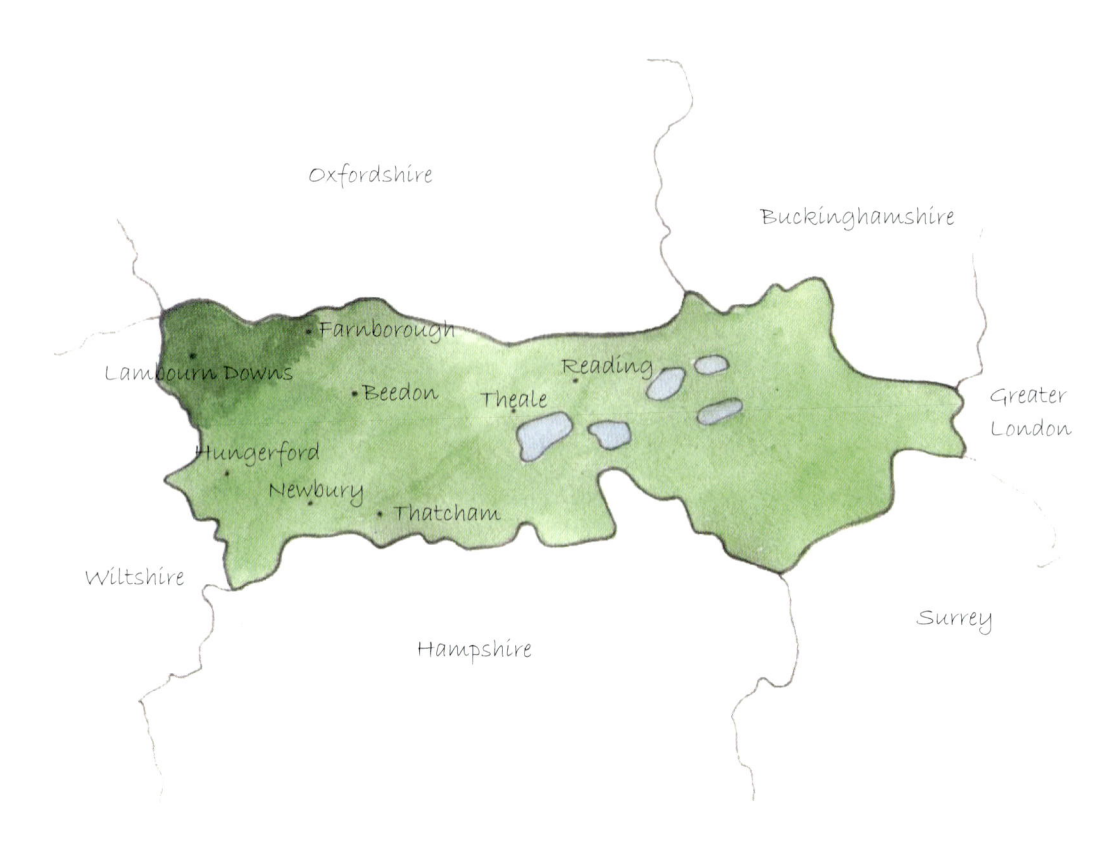

Beedon Barrow, Beedon.
There was an attempt many years ago to open this Barrow, which caused a most spectacular thunderstorm, this made the hopeful treasure seekers beat a hasty retreat from the site. It is supposed to contain a golden coffin and is also well known as a Faerie site.

Grims Ditches.
This is a series of linear earthworks that lie along the County border starting from the south east of Wantage in Oxfordshire, there are also many Barrows close at hand.
The name Grim is derived from the Anglo Saxon War God, Grim is associated with the devil and goblins.

The entrance to Faerie hills may be found by walking nine times around it at the time of a full moon.

To protect your home on Midsummer's Eve the night when evil spirits are about make a garland of St Johns Wort, Plantain, Corn Marigold, Yarrow and Ivy and then burn it on the evening fire.

FAERIE PLANTS

Clover: A four leafed clover apart from being lucky, gives second sight and the ability to see Faeries.
It will also break a Faerie spell.

Cowslips: Especially protected by the Faeries and is used in Faerie magic. Can be used to find Faerie treasure.

Blackberries: The fruit is very popular with Faeries.

Bluebells: This is the most potent plant for magic. If you plant them in your garden it will attract Faeries. If you hear one ringing it indicates the presence of an evil spirit and possibly your own death knell. For this reason it is known as Deadmans Bells in Scotland.

Daisies: To the Celts Daisies were the spirits of all the children who had died at birth so it was considered extremely unlucky to damage or step on a Daisy, as they believed that their own children would not thrive if they did so.
Putting a daisy chain around a child's neck protects it from being carried off by the Faeries.

Foxglove: The flower is used in Faerie magic, the leaves are used to gain release from enchantments. If planted in your garden it is an invitation for them to enter. In the north of England the bad Faeries would give the flowers to the Foxes to wear on their paws so that they could sneak around more quietly while they were hunting. The white markings inside the flowers are the Faeries fingerprints.

FAERIE PLANTS

Goldenrod: Underneath this magical plant Faeries bury their treasure. Grow it by your back door and it will bring good luck
It can also be used for divining to find underground springs.

Heather: The stalks of the plants are used as Faerie food and a field of Heather may be hiding a portal to the Faerie Kingdom.

Holly, Hollyhock, Lavender and Lilacs are also great favourites.

Morning Glory: If planted by the gate in your garden will keep out the malicious kind of Faeries.

St Johns Wort: This flower was used in the Celtic Midsummer Festival, symbolising the sun.
It provides protection against Faeries and is useful in breaking spells. It has also been used in healing.

Herb Bennet: Hang the roots (which smell of cloves) by the door and these will keep evil spirits away.

Pansy or Heartsease: In Midsummer Night's Dream, Oberon squeezes the juice of this Pansy into Titania's eyes so that she will fall in love with Bottom.

Primroses: These plants give the Faeries invisibility, if they are eaten you will see them. Hang a bunch on your door and it will act as an invitation; to keep them away, sprinkle the petals outside the door.

Thyme: Wear a sprig of this and you will see Faeries. Sprinkling Thyme on the front step will invite them in.
Wild Thyme gathered from the side of a Faerie mound is a potent ingredient for Faerie magic.
It is dangerous to bring it into the house.

Wiltshire

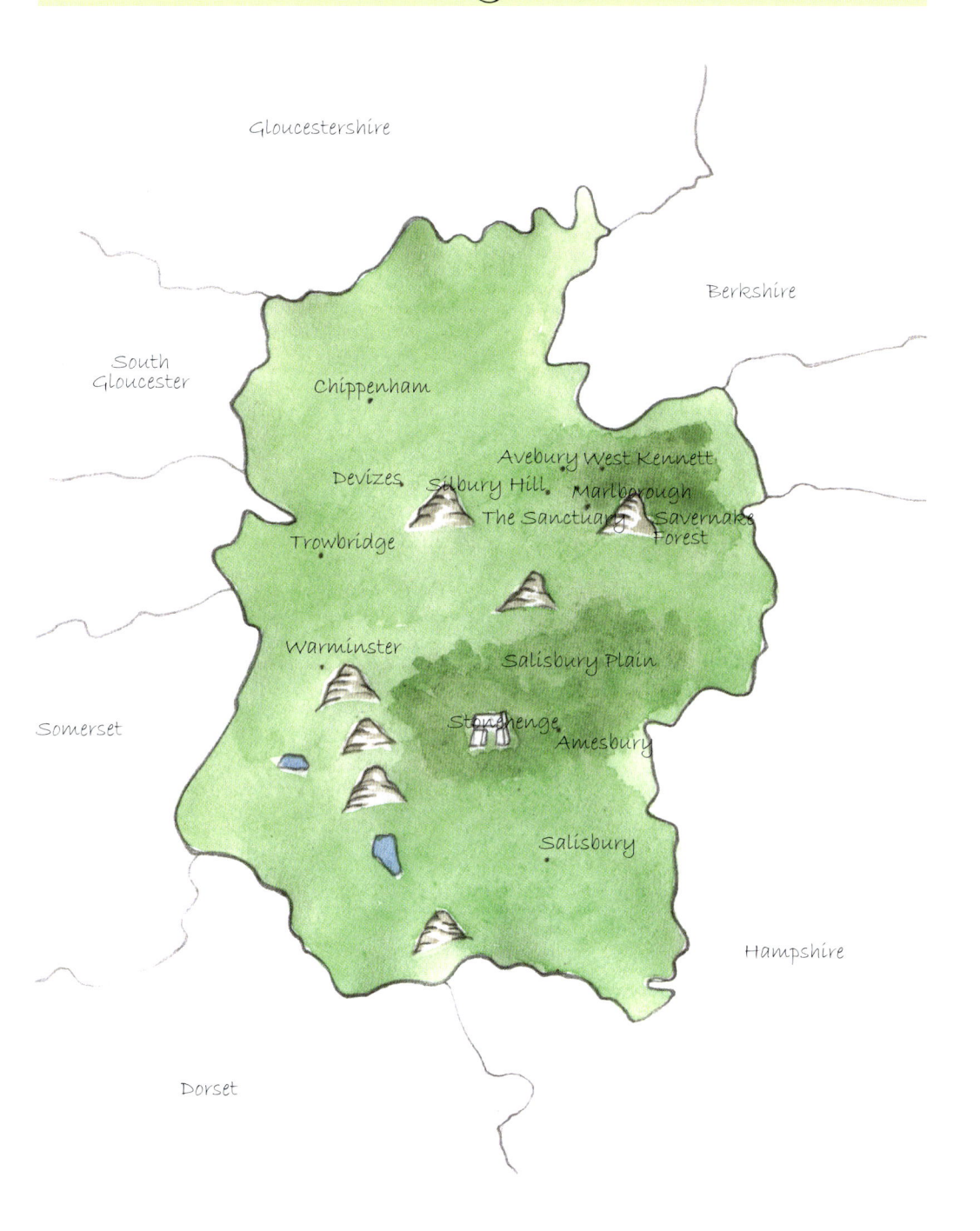

Gloucestershire

Berkshire

South Gloucester

Chippenham

Avebury West Kennett
Devizes   Marlborough
Silbury Hill
The Sanctuary   Savernake Forest

Trowbridge

Warminster

Salisbury Plain

Stonehenge   Amesbury

Somerset

Salisbury

Hampshire

Dorset

Wiltshire

The stone circle near the village of Avebury has been the site of many strange happenings.
Small bands of Faeries have been seen dancing around the main stone circle of this ancient monument in the moonlight, and lights and music have been seen by people driving past at night.
Two wide avenues of stones lead from this site, one to the west and one to the south.
The southern avenue leads to the Sanctuary on Overton Hill, this is another ancient site which consists of two circles of stone.

Hackpen Hill Barrow, Avebury.
This is a Faerie hill where a shepherd boy once became lost. The Faeries took care of the boy and showed him their underground halls. He stayed with them for a while entranced by their music before returning to the upper world and his flock of sheep.

The Devil's Chair.
This huge stone is 14 ft wide by 13 ft high, It used to be visited at Beltane by the local girls.
They would sit upon the ledge and make wishes.

West Kennet, Longbarrow.
Many offerings are left at this barrow for the Faeries and earth spirits.

Faerie lights can be seen hovering over the stones on dark nights.

If you bury a wand made of willow or hazel beneath a Faerie barrow or fort this will summon the Faeries.

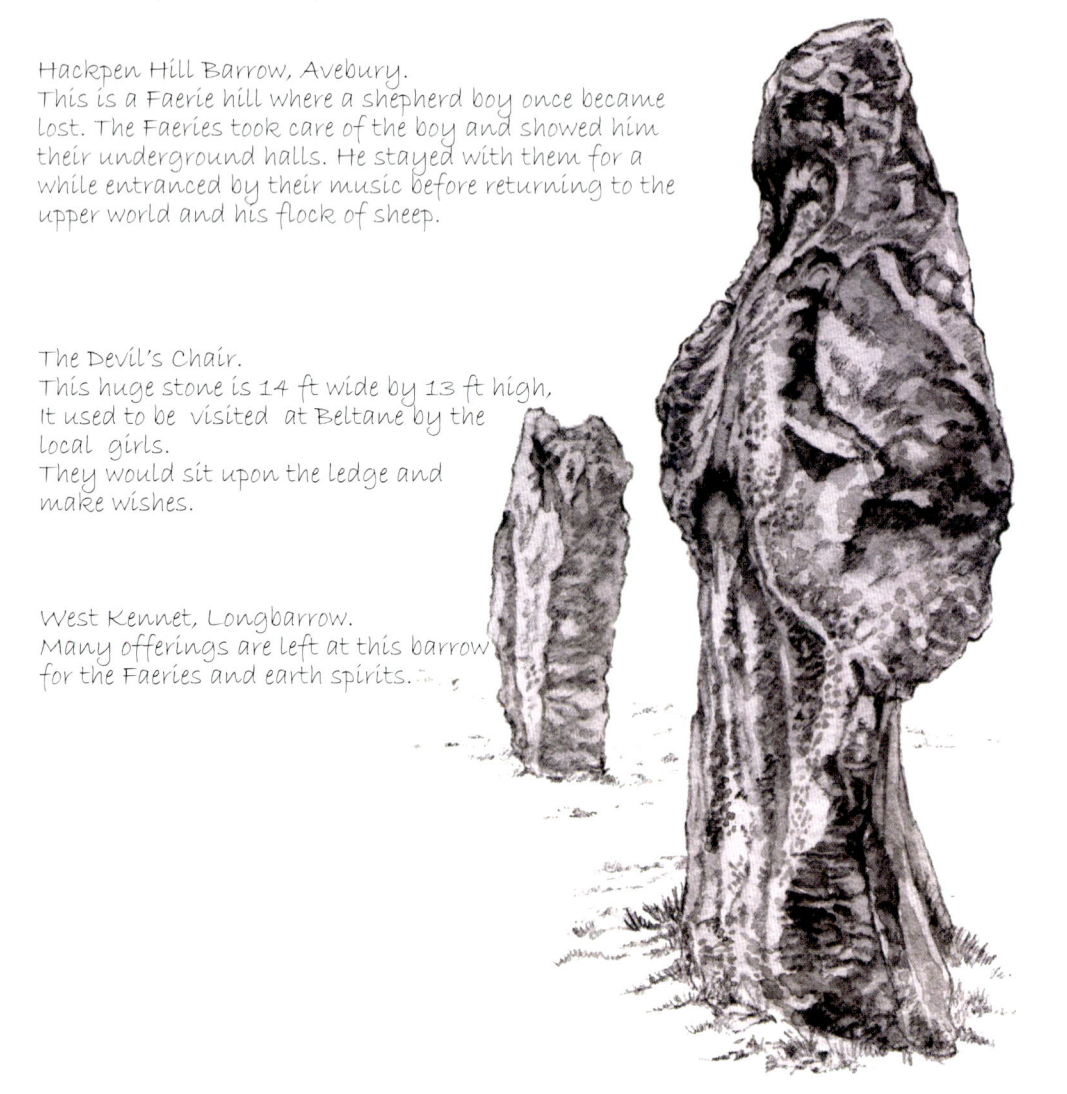

OXFORDSHIRE

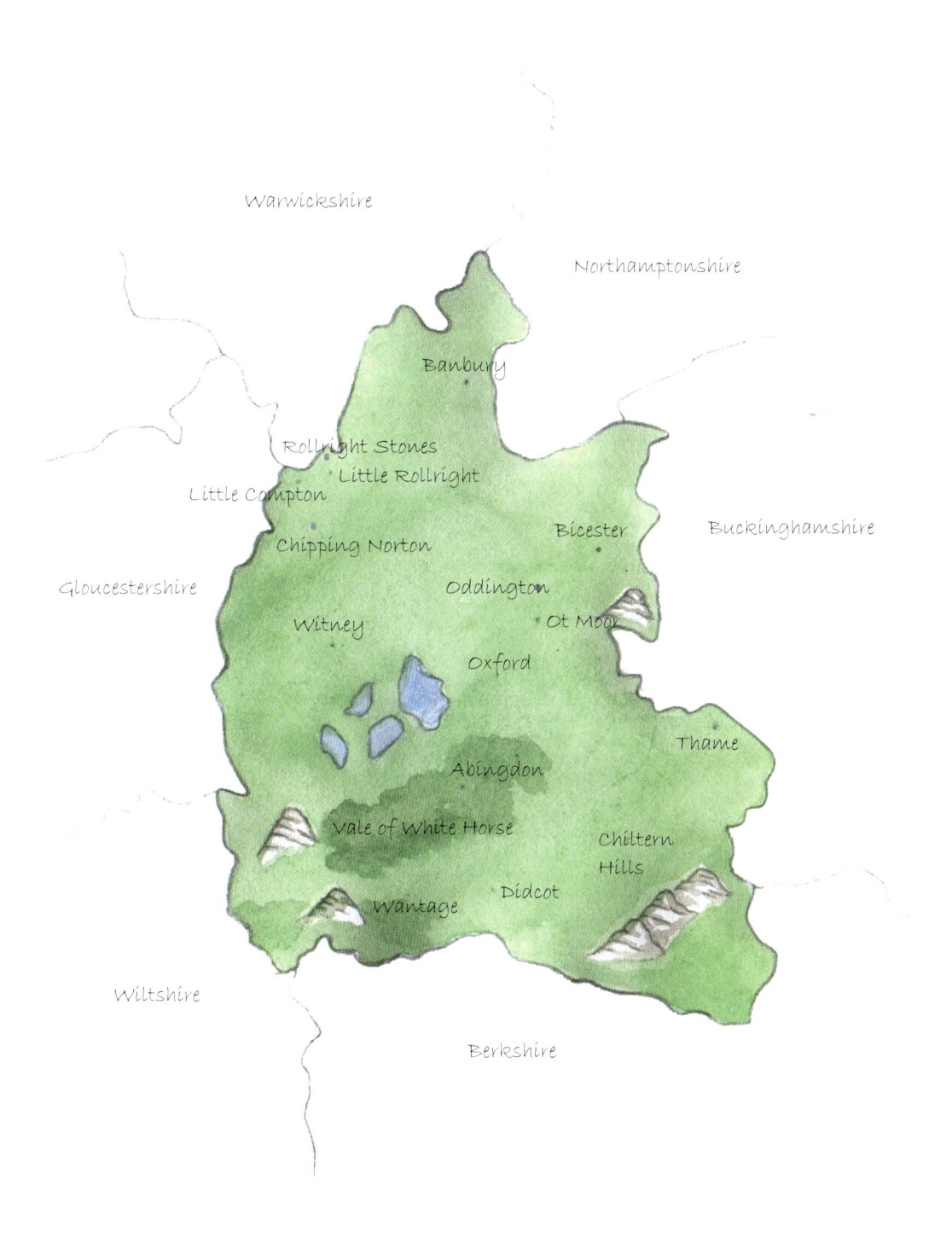

OXFORDSHIRE

The Rollright Stones.
A Bronze Age site, the stones are widely believed to be a King and his Army that were turned to stone by a local Witch.
The circle of stones is a 100 ft in diameter, to one side stands the King stone.
This was a conquering army that marched as far north as Little Rollright until the King came upon a local wise woman.
She told the King that if he could see Long Compton within seven strides he would be King of the whole country.
Taking the seven steps up the hill his view was obscured by a mound, jubilant, the Witch turned the King and all his men to stone.
And there they still stand waiting for somebody who has enough strong magic to break the spell.

The Witch then turned herself into an Elder tree close to the stones to stand guard against the spell being broken.

This site is also a favourite spot of the Oxfordshire Faeries.
At certain times of the year, at the full moon, the stones will come to life and perform strange dances with the Faeries. Then they will dance down to a nearby spring for a drink to quench their thirst.

A magical faerie ointment if rubbed into the eyes will allow mortals to see the faeries.

Ot Moor: This is an area of flat swampy ground east of Oxford. It has been known as an area of bewitchment and ancient magic for many years.
The black peaty water of the Moor has many medicinal benefits. There are several wells; the one at Oddington will cure Moor evil, a disease which affects cattle.
The waters from the others cure skin and eye problems.

Many years ago it used to be the custom for the locals to visit the stones on Midsummer Eve and cut the Elder. The tree was then supposed to bleed and bring fertility to the land for the year ahead.

BUCKINGHAMSHIRE

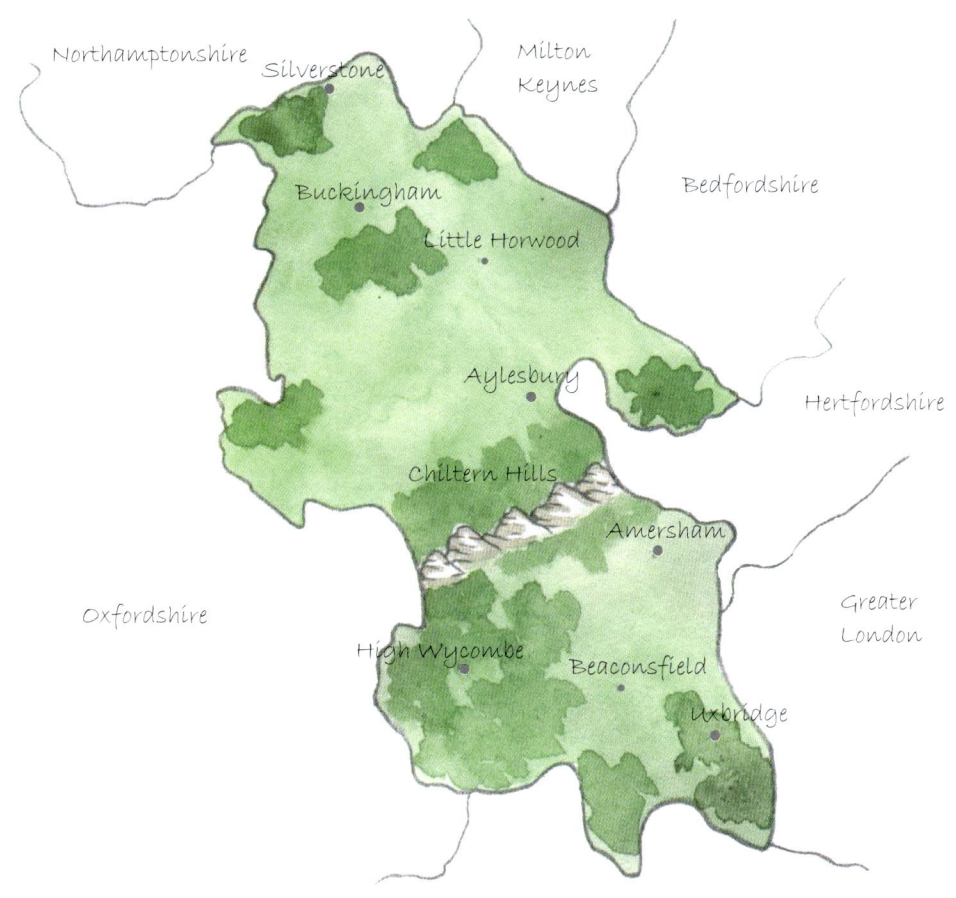

Shucklow Warren, Little Horwood:
The Saxons used to call this site Scuccan Hlgew which means the Goblins Barrow and even now the area is avoided and the Goblins feared.
Goblins are evil creatures and are best avoided, they are also great shapeshifters and can turn themselves into any wild animal that they choose but their favourites are owls and bats.

Mildew on crops and canker on rose bushes are Faerie blights.
Faerie ladies often disguise themselves as white doves, mice or toads.

Suffolk

Suffolk

The Wolf Pit Children.
Many years ago labourers were working in the fields on the edge of the village of Woolpit in Suffolk when they saw two strange looking children coming from the Old Wolf pits (These were ancient trenches near the village which had been used to trap wolves and wild beasts)
The boy and girl were strangely dressed and they both had a strange green tinge to their skin.
They did not speak any language that the men could understand and they were both obviously scared and confused.
At the end of the day the men took the children home to the village. At first the two children would eat nothing they were offered except for green beans, this went on for days until finally they began to eat a more normal diet. As soon as they did so their skin lost the green tinge and they began to look more like normal children.
The longer the children stayed in the village the more words they picked up until finally they could tell the villagers that they had come from the " The Land of St Martin". It was a land of gloomy twilight separated from it's sunny neighbouring country by a wide river. While the two children had been tending their Father's flock of sheep there had been a tremendous noise and the children had lost consciousness, when they had come to, they found themselves in the Wolf Pits. Although the villagers and the children searched for the way back into The Land of St Martin they never managed to find it.
So the children stayed in the village of Woolpit. After a while the boy sickened and died but the girl survived. She later married a man from Lynn, Norfolk. Nothing else has been recorded of her fate or of the whereabouts of The Land of St Martins.

Stowmarket: Faeries can sometimes be seen dancing in a ring in the Meadows that border the road between Stowmarket and Bury St Edmunds. 3 ft high and sparkling from head to toe.

Malekin: This little creature haunts the castle of Dagworthy. She is a human child stolen by the Faeries and is still desperately trying to regain her freedom.

Humans are not always taken to Faerieland for ever, sometimes they are just 'borrowed' for the night to carry out chores for the Faeries while they are still sleeping.
They will be returned before the morning and wake up knowing nothing of their nightly labours, except for the aching muscles and dishpan hands.

FAERIE TREES

Hazel:
The Well of Wisdom otherwise known as Connla's Well in Tipperary Ireland, stands at the centre of the Celtic Otherworld. From here flows the water which feeds all other sacred wells and springs throughout the rest of the world.
Overhanging this well grows a sacred Hazel tree which produces the nine nuts of poetic art and wisdom, these nuts fall into the water and are eaten by Fintan the salmon of knowledge.
When the nuts fall into the water bubbles of inspiration rise to the surface which with the husks then float down the five streams that flow from this well spreading the wisdom to the rest of the world.
The Hazel tree has been considered a magical tree for many hundreds of years and to the Celts it was known as the Sacred Tree of Knowledge and it's nuts treasured, believing them to be the food of the Gods.
It was not just the nuts that they valued but also the wood itself from which they made wands, using them in magical ceremonies and for divination.
The power of the wand has been recognised by Pagans and Christians alike, for example it was with a Hazel wand that St Patrick drove the snakes out of Ireland.
Along with the wands which are still used by the modern day Druid, Hazel dowsing rods are commonly used to find underground springs, although in Cornwall they are also used to locate mineral deposits.

Great care has to be taken to cut the wands or dowsings rods at the the correct time.
Midsummer's Eve is the best time as the Hazel tree is at its most powerful then.

The smaller more flexible branches of the tree are woven into hats, placed upon the head they can then be used to make wishes.
Sailors also wore these hats as protection against storms.

This belief in the power of the Hazel was and is still wide spread throughout Britain; in the more remote parts of the country it is still a custom for Brides to be presented with bags of nuts upon leaving the church to encourage fertility in their marriage.

Hawthorn:
A grove of Hawthorn trees is a good place to spot Faeries, in fact all thorn trees are used as a meeting place for Faerie folk.
If a fire is started using thorn wood on top of a Faerie mound it will force the occupants to return a stolen child.

An old spring custom is to plait crowns of the blossom and leave them for the Faeries.

FAERIE TREES

Oak:
According to the Celts the Oak was the Father of the Trees and worshipped in vast groves of them, these formed their holy shrines. They revered the Oak above all other trees because of the powerful magic that the tree contained and it was used in many of their celebrations and rituals. The name Druid means 'Knowing the Oak'.

Oak Apples: The galls on Oak trees are caused by the larvae of a certain type of wasp and these galls were used to find out if a child had been bewitched. Three of the galls would have been plucked from the Oak and thrown into a bucket of water. The bucket would then have been placed underneath the child's cradle. If the galls float then the child is safe but if they sink it means the child is bewitched. All of this must be done in silence otherwise it will not work.

Yew:
This is an ancient sacred tree which can live for anything up to 3000 years, its evergreen leaves a symbol of mourning and resurrection. Many Yew trees can be found planted in graveyards, and small sprigs of Yew were often placed in the grave to protect the spirit.

One old tale that is told about the Yew is that the tree became dissatisfied with it's dark green needles envying the other trees in the forest their beautiful coloured leaves. It grumbled to the Faeries asking them to change its appearance, so to keep the Yew happy they changed its leaves into gold. The golden leaves glittered in the sun but this attracted the thieves and they stripped the tree bare. The Faeries then gave the tree delicate leaves of crystal but a storm came and the rain smashed the delicate leaves leaving the tree naked.

The tree was then clothed in bright green and gold leaves that fluttered in the wind but this attracted all the wild animals of the woods, and the tree was again stripped bare of its leaves. The Yew tree stood there in the wood and moaned for its own evergreen leaves to be returned so the Faeries once again did their magic and returned the Yew tree to its original form, but because the tree still envied the other trees their colourful leaves the Faeries gave it bright red berries to wear every year, and made the berries along with the leaves poisonous to discourage the beasts of the forest.

Elder:
If you stand beneath an Elder tree on Midsummer's Eve you will see the King of the Faeries and his entourage but be careful you do not get swept away to Faerieland.

Elder wood is greatly prized by the Faeries so do not use it for a cradle or the baby will be pinched black and blue.

The Elder Mother guards the tree and although she is usually kind she can become dangerous if her trees are harmed so you must always ask permission before cutting an Elder tree.
"Ourd gal, give me some of thy wood
An oi will give some of moine
When oi grows inter a tree"

Do not bring Elder into the house or burn it as it is very unlucky and it will bring the Devil into the house.

Never drive your cattle with sticks of Elder or beat your children with one as they will never prosper!

FAERIE TREES

As mentioned before on page 30 The Apple Tree Man is the guardian of Orchards.
To ensure future crops the last few apples would be left for him and the Pixies.

Apple:
The magical properties of the Apple tree were recognised by the Celts who used them in their Samhain festivals.
Great care was taken of the trees by the Celts, wassailing them at the turn of every season to ensure good crops, for they believed that the apple was the the fruit of the Gods. Blessings and prayers were said in the orchards and hot spiced cider drunk in toast to the trees.
Anything left over in the wassailing bowl would be poured over the roots of the trees as a tribute to the spirit of the trees.
"Old Apple Tree we wassail thee, and happily thou wilt bear, For the Lord knows where we shall be , Till apples another year...."
Two customs that are left over from the Samhain festival and are still in practice today are the dunking for apples in a barrel and peeling an apple in front of a mirror to see an image of your future partner.
May Eve is the traditional time to plant new trees, place a piece of coal beneath the roots, then water with cider.

Rowan:
Use it as a protection against Faerie spells.
Dairy maids used it as a charm to stop butter from spoiling when being churned.
Branches of Rowan hung about houses and outbuildings will bring good luck.
Every croft in Scotland would have had its own Rowan tree planted outside for protection. Red ribbons would be tied to the fruiting branches to keep witches from the door.

FAERIE TREES

The Holly is a sacred tree to the Druids as the evergreen leaves symbolise immortality. It was the Celtic custom to gather branches of Holly and Ivy and take them into the home during the winter months to symbolise that life and growth would return again in the spring. This also gave shelter to Faeries and Elves during the cold weather, in return for this kindness they would cause no mischief, in fact bringing good luck into the mortals home.

The Celts believed that it was unlucky to chop a Holly tree down or to burn the wood so the branches would have been carefully pulled off to prevent damaging it. Probably from a tree growing close to the house as most homes had a Holly planted nearby to ward off evil spirits.
However all branches and leaves had to be removed from the house by Imbolc Eve (31st January) for any leaf left inside would encourage the nastier Faerie folk like Goblins to remain in the house.

A small branch of Holly would have been kept from the festivities and hung outside the house for protection against lightning.

At Yuletide place a lighted candle on a Holly leaf floating in a bowl of water, make a wish and if the leaf floats then your wish will come true.

To see the image of your future partner in your dreams, pick nine leaves at midnight on a Friday and sleep with them under your pillow.

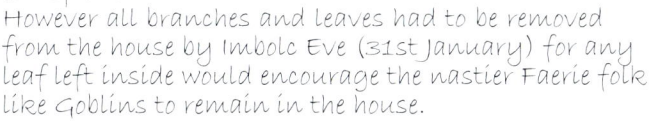

CAMBRIDGESHIRE

CAMBRIDGSHIRE

Until the Fens were drained there were many tales Of the Jack 'O' Lantern (Will of the Wisp, Lantern Men).
These glistening lights would seek out the lone traveller and lure him into the marshes at night. Flickering lights would dance across the water, showing false paths and inviting the traveller to take a false step to a watery end.
It is not a good idea to whistle in the Fens at night as this will attract the Jack 'O' Lantern. If he does come the best idea is to lay flat on your face until the light passes on over the top of you.

West Wratting:
The countryside between West Wratting and Balsham is the territory of a creature known locally as the Shug Monkey. It is a jet black shaggy haired thing with staring eyes in a monkey face.

Yallery Brown: A nasty cruel little creature that will sleep for years curled up under a rock, its scrawny wrinkled little body wrapped up tightly in its own beard.

A Farmer heard the sound of whimpering coming from nearby so he followed the sound and found Yallery Brown crying under his rock.
The sprite promised to stay with the Farmer for ever and help him with his work, as long as he never thanked him.
The kind hearted man took him home and gave him a meal, but from then on he began to regret his kindness, for Yallery Brown's help turned out to be bad luck. His neighbours saw the work being done by invisible hands so they started avoiding the Farmer and he became so unpopular that in an effort to get rid of the sprite he thanked him for his work. But Yallery's evil nature came out, from then on he ruined everything the Farmer did.
Singing taunting songs,
"Loss and mischance and Yallery Brown
You've let out yourself from under the stone".
The poor Farmer was never rid of him and he died penniless and alone.

Tiddy Ones, Tiddy Men Tiddy People.
These are the Fen peoples nature spirits, the most well known is The Tiddy Mun who is called upon to withdraw the waters when the Fens flood.

Hyster Sprites:
East Anglian and Lincolnshire Faeries, small Sandy coloured with green eyes. Other names include 'Yarthkins' and 'Strangers'.

Black Shuck: These are black demon dogs that are quite a talking point in the Fens.
It can be as big as a calf with red glowing eyes.
It loiters on lonely roads and in grave yards, hiding in the mists rising off the marshes. If you feel its breath upon your neck do not be tempted to turn around as sight of Black Shuck means death to you or your family.

Herefordshire

A Herefordshire mother, many years ago, was very worried about her young son, it was very ugly although it had been a beautiful baby at birth. It wouldn't grow no matter how much it was fed, and it never stirred from its cot.
This went on for many years until her son came home on leave from the army, he took one look at the child laying in its cot and realised that it was a changeling and that his baby brother had been taken by the Faeries.
So after taking advice from the local wise woman he started to prepare two emptied eggshells which he filled with malt and hops.
These were carefully placed over the fire in a pan. The baby watched the Soldier with great interest, and when the mixture began to boil, started to laugh declaring that although he had lived for a thousand years he had never seen beer brewed in eggshells before.
The changeling then realised he had been tricked into revealing his true identity and flew quickly out of the window before the Soldier could catch him.
Within minutes the real son walked into the house much to the delight of his Mother and Brother.

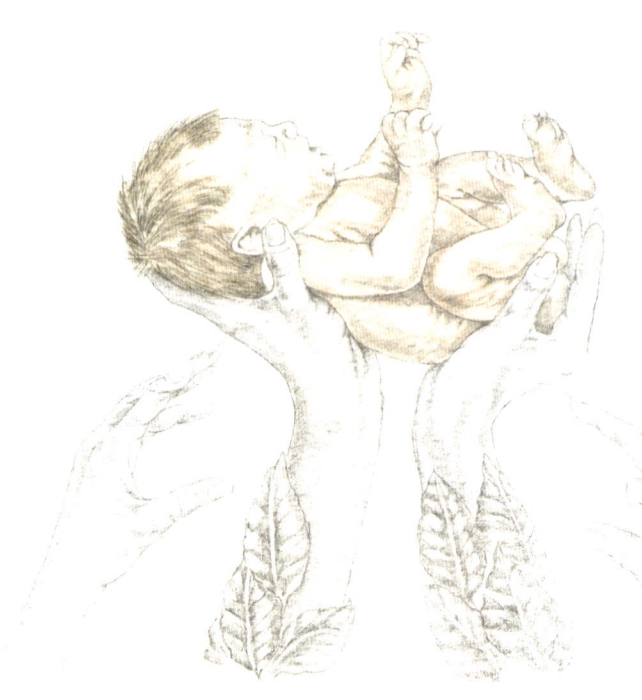

The original theory of Ley Lines came from Alfred Watkins in 1925. He believed that invisible lines of power circled the earth.
He observed that many sacred places and natural sites could be linked together (tumuli, faerie places, standing stones stone circles and sacred sites).
By ruling a straight line through many of them on a map he thought he proved the existence of these leys. At least five places must be able to be linked to qualify for a ley line and where the lines cross over this is called a Ley Centre. At least seven lines must radiate from this point. These Ley Centres have a very strong magical energy and magnetic field.
Many important pagan sites are built over these centres such as Stonehenge and Avebury.

I have noted one strong ley line while lying in bed one night poring over a map, that radiated out from one sacred site, and as my husband kindly pointed out there was an amazing amount of little chefs situated along it! This obviously proves that the planners of these sites are in tune with their inner mystical beings.

GNOMES

Gnomes: They are Earth spirits that live beneath Oak trees, in woods or caves. They spend their time caring for the trees and animals, and guard the treasures of the Earth.

The average Gnome has a very long life span and can live for up to a thousand years. They are also wonderful metal workers, especially with swords and armour.

Many statues of Gnomes are found in gardens around the country, they are more than just a garden ornament. All those little red capped men are there as a protective symbol for your garden!

There was a Gnome family who lived in a mill alongside the Miller and his family. In exchange for milk and cornmeal the Gnomes kept watch over the mill and helped alongside the Miller when he was extra busy. The Father Gnome was also very skilled with herbs which was useful whenever the Miller's family became ill. With the Gnomes help the family became very prosperous and many of their neighbours became jealous and spread rumours that the Miller was dabbling in Black Magic to gain his riches. One little girl knew better however, she knew that a family of Gnomes lived with the Miller and his family and that they were responsible for the Good Luck. So she made a model of one the Gnomes, painted it and set it in the garden of her home. Although her parents and friends made fun of the statue she kept it there amongst the flowers. The Gnomes at the Mill heard of the statue and went to the garden to have a look, and they were so touched that the little girl had wanted a statue of them that they decided to reward her. So each month she received a small gold coin and as time went on her family became so well off that their neighbours decided to put a small Gnome statue in their gardens as well as it obviously brought good luck.

WALES

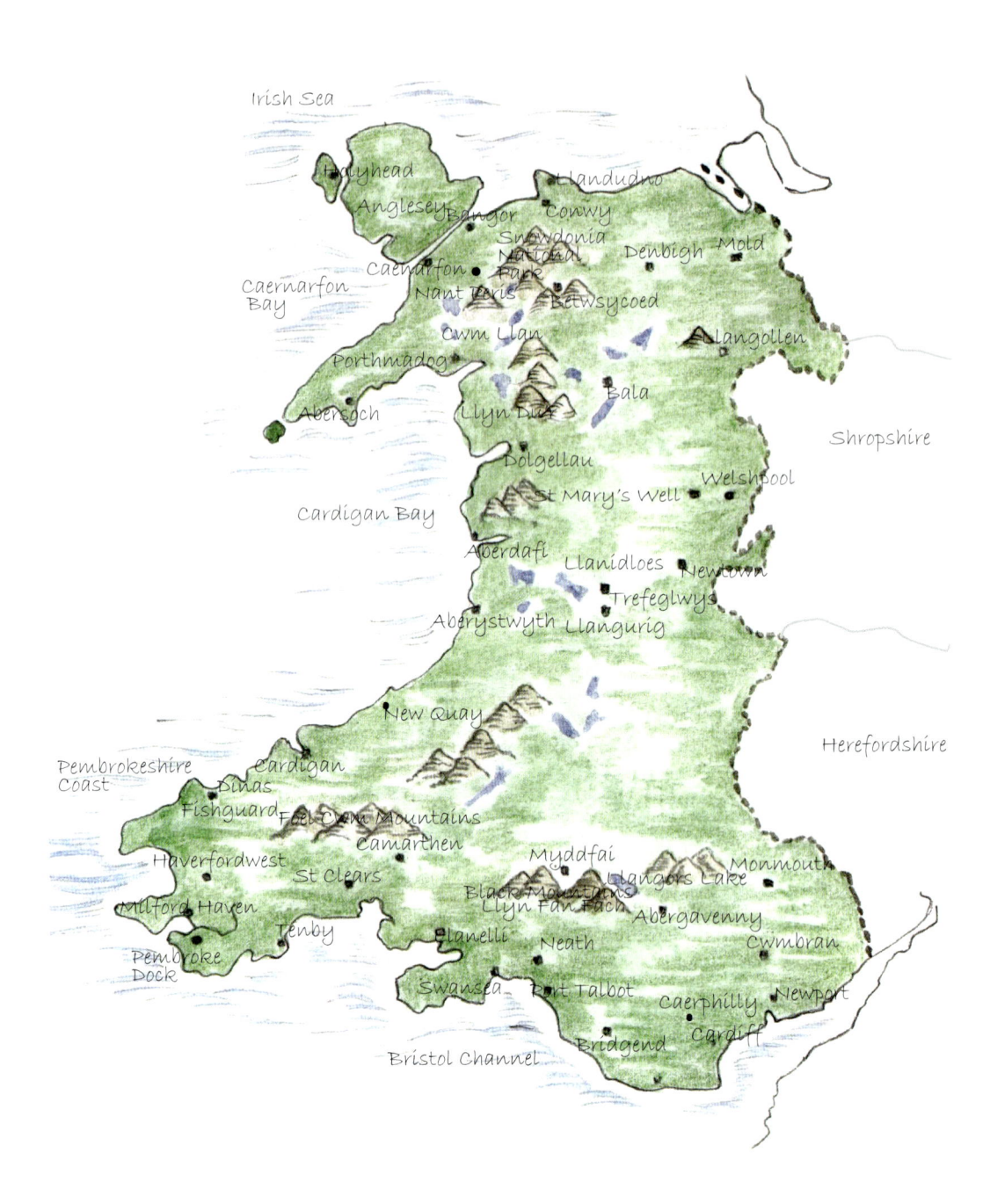

WALES

Coblynau: Welsh Mine Goblin, cousins to the Cornish Knockers. They are often seen working at the seam faces, if you are lucky enough to see one it means that a rich seam of ore is present.

Ellyllon: Welsh Elves; They are tiny gossamer creatures that live on toadstools and faerie butter (a fungoid substance found in the roots of old Oaks). The Queen of the Ellyllon is Mab.

Gwyllion: X These are evil mountain faeries, who are mainly women. The majority of them are extremely ugly and they take great pleasure in waiting for the unwary traveller on the lonely mountain passes.
They are friends and patrons of the Goat and often mimic them in their appearance.
They fear Iron (as most Faeries do), sunlight but also storms.

Fair Family or Fair Folk

The family of Pellings from Betws Garman (Gwynedd) are the descendants of a marriage between a family member and a faerie called Penelope.
She agreed to marry her sweetheart only if he promised never to strike her with iron.
They lived happily for many years until she was accidentally hit by a bridle as her husband was harnessing the family pony. Penelope vanished, never to be seen again.

Two fiddlers Twn and Ned plus the piper Dic were enticed into Yr Ugof Ddu, the black cave near Criccieth by a group of Faeries.
They were never seen again but their music can still be heard coming from the depths of the caves.

Virtous Well, Trellech, Gwent: Originally called St Anne's Well, well known for the healing virtues of its water.
To make a wish in this well drop a pebble into the water, if bubbles rise to the surface then your wish will be granted, if not then I am afraid you will be unlucky and not receive your wish.

WALES

The Green Lady of Caerphilly:
Haunts lonely ruins and takes on the appearance of ivy.

Verry Volk:
The Faeries of Gower, are very small and dress in scarlet and green

Plant Rhys Pwfen (plant hree thoorn):
A family name for a tribe of faerie people who live on a small invisible island. The island stays this way because of a certain magical herb that grows there.
They are very handsome, but some what shorter than average. One of their customs is to attend the local market in Cardigan and mingle with the humans. They pay good prices for all their goods and are honest and pleasant to all who have dealings with them.

Tylwyth Teg (terlooeth terg): The Fair Family.
They are a golden haired people who love dancing and making faerie rings. Their dwellings are underground or underwater. The faerie girls are easily won as wives and will live with their mortal husbands quite happily while it suits them.
They hand out many rich gifts to their mortal friends but these will vanish if ever spoken of.

Bendith y Mamau (ben dith uh momay) Mothers Blessing, which is the name of the faeries in Carmarthenshire, this saying became popular as a way to ward of harm.
They live beneath lakes, on Faerie Islands or underground in beautiful palaces.
One of the more unpleasant sides to them is the habit of stealing small children and replacing them with their own changelings known as crimbils.
It is thought that they need to improve their blood line with mortal children. Too many years of inbreeding!

A small cottage in Trefeglwys was the place of much trouble between a husband and wife. They were constantly arguing about their twins, who the mother was convinced had been swapped for faerie changelings.
A local Wizard was called in to advise them.
An eggshell was to be boiled and made into a stew which then had to given to the farm workers for dinner.
If the twins said or did anything unusual then it was certain that they were faerie changelings, and then should be thrown into the Llyn Ebyr Lake.
As soon as the shell began to boil they started to chant
"Acorns before Oak I saw,
An Egg before a Hen,
But never one hen's egg stew
Enough for harvest men".

With this the mother took them straight to the lake and threw them in.
A group of faeries immediately appeared to save them from drowning. They handed back the stolen children and then disappeared back into the hills.

WALES

Bedd Taliesin, Ceulan-y-maes-mawr, Dyfed:
If a mortal sleeps in this Cairn they will wake up as either an idiot or poet.

Llyn Barfog, Gwynedd:
A local farmer was rewarded for a service to the Faeries with a gift of a magical Cow which gave an endless supply of milk. He was very pleased with his gift, until the Cow grew old and her milk supply dwindled until eventually she gave no more.
The farmer did not wish to keep the cow now that it was useless, so the following day he decided that he would slaughter the animal and sell the meat in the local market.
Before he could do so the Faeries called to the Cow from Llyn Barfour the nearby lake. The Cow heard the call and trotted off eagerly to the water's edge.
A green clothed Faerie rose from the water and took the cow back down to the Faerie realm below.

Maen Llia, nr Ystradfellte, Powys:

This Bronze age marker stone is twelve feet tall and two feet thick. Stones of this shape are very unusual and this one is supposed to drink from the River Nedd when ever it hears a cock crow.

Bryn Y Ellyllon, Mold, Clywd.
The Hills of the Goblins.
Goblins chased away some foolhardy miners from their hills to protect their gold, and at the same time put a dreadful curse on them. The Miners were all dead within the year.
The Goblins share their Barrow with a huge golden hued ghost. The skeleton of a large man wrapped in a golden cape was found in a grave here. Surrounding the body were hundreds of Amber beads.
Most of the treasure is now in the British Museum.

St Non's Well, St Davids, Dyfed.
The best day for the healing powers of the well to work is the 1st of March, which is St David's Day.
Throw offerings into the water or leave them at the side of the well.
Up until the 1800's children were still being immersed into the water to cure their ailments.

WALES

St Mary's Well, Ffynnon Fair, Llanfair, Caerinion, Powys:
The waters from this well was used as a cure for rheumatism but it could also be used as protection against Faerie magic.

The cave of Tangrogo at Denbigh is inhabited by three Faerie sisters, although they are never seen, their footprints are often found around the cave.

Bwbachod: Welsh Brownies, they are friendly and very hardworking although they are said to hate teetotallers!

Pentre Ifan, Fishguard, Dyfed:
This megalithic structure which is also known as The Womb of Cerridwen, is a haunt of the Tylweth Teg.

A Faerie path travels across Cardigan Bay underneath the water.
When the water is clear and calm, little figures can be seen scuttling back and forth along this path.

Nymphs have a special liking for children, especially those left unattended or abandoned or illegitimate.
They will take them away to raise them as their own, and the child may be replaced with a weak nymph changeling.
To avoid them taking newborn babies, food must be left for them especially honey for forty days after the birth.

Gwarwyn-A-Throt: Welsh version of the Faerie of the To-Tit-Tot type.

Also Trwtyn-Tratyn

WALES

Cwn Annwn: X Hounds of the Otherworlds. Welsh phantom dogs which are seen as a death omen. Their growling is louder when at a distance and becomes softer as they draw nearer.

Ellylldon: A Welsh spirit similar to the English Will O the Wisp, it appears as a light and misleads travellers from their path.

Gwragedd Annwn: Welsh water fairies, beautiful golden haired lake maidens who occasionally take mortals for husbands. These Faeries are kind to mothers and also to children.

The surname of Morgan comes from the meaning born of the sea.

There was belief among the locals of Milford Haven that the Sea Faeries used to visit their market via a secret passage that led from the sea bed.

A young farmer was tending to his animals on the shore of a lake near Myddfai when he saw a beautiful lake maiden on the water. Falling in love with her immediately, he attracted her attention by offering her some barley bread. "Hard baked is thy bread, 'Tis not so easy to catch me" she called to him.
The next day she was there again and this time he offered her some unbaked dough. "Moist is thy bread, I don't want thee".
The third day he hurried back to the lake's edge carrying some lightly baked bread. This she accepted and then instantly disappeared below the waters of the lake.
Just as the farmer was turning away disappointed, she reappeared with her father and identical twin sister. The father told the hopeful suitor that if he could correctly identify the girl he wished to marry then he would give his consent.
The young farmer was horrified, the two were identical, as he hesitated, one of the girls moved her foot slightly and he realised that must be his sweetheart.

WALES

A mermaid was often seen laying on a rock called Carreg Ina, near New Quay. She was usually avoided by the local Fisherman until one day she became entangled in their nets. They did not dare leave her in case she cursed them so they carefully released her from the nets. The Mermaid was so grateful that she warned the Fisherman of an impending storm and told them to set sail for the Harbour straight away. This they did and had just moored their boats when a fierce storm hit the coastline, all the other Fishermen at sea that day, who had not been lucky enough to hear the Mermaid's warning were drowned.

Cwm y Llan : south east of Snowdon, Gwynedd:
This is one of the many places that the Tylwyth Teg are said to inhabit. They were spotted many years ago by a Shepherd who set free one of little people who had become trapped underneath a fallen rock. The grateful Tylweth Teg presented him with a walking stick, which turned out to be a lucky gift for the Shepherd. From then on every ewe in his flock had two healthy ewe lambs. Unfortunately after many years of good luck he lost his prized walking stick in a flood and his good fortune disappeared with it.

Llyn Du'r Arddu (The Black Lake of Arddu) on the north side of Snowdon.
This Lake is haunted and there are many tales of Faeries and Goblins dancing on the shore of the Lake.

Llyn Fawr, north of the Rhondda Valley, Mid Glamorgan:
It is supposed to be impossible to throw a stone into the Lake as invisible Faerie hands will catch it. Sometimes the Lady of the Lake is visible combing her hair near the edge of the water.

St Lythan's Cromlech, Dyffryn, near Cardiff, South Glamorgan:
The field in which this impressive Cromlech stands is known as the Accursed Field as nothing will grow here.
The hole through the centre of the stone is where the Spirits of the dead fly through. On Midsummer Eve the stone on the top of the Cromlech spins around three times and a wish made here on Halloween will come true.

Faerie Rings in Wales are called Cylchau Tylwyth Teg.

St Peris's Well, Nant Peris, Llanberis Pass, Gwynedd:
This is another healing well, but this time one with a difference.
There is a large eel living in the water of this well, and to be cured of any ills, you have to bathe with it.
If the eel wraps itself around you when you are in the water you will be cured. (One bather apparently died of fright when it did so.)

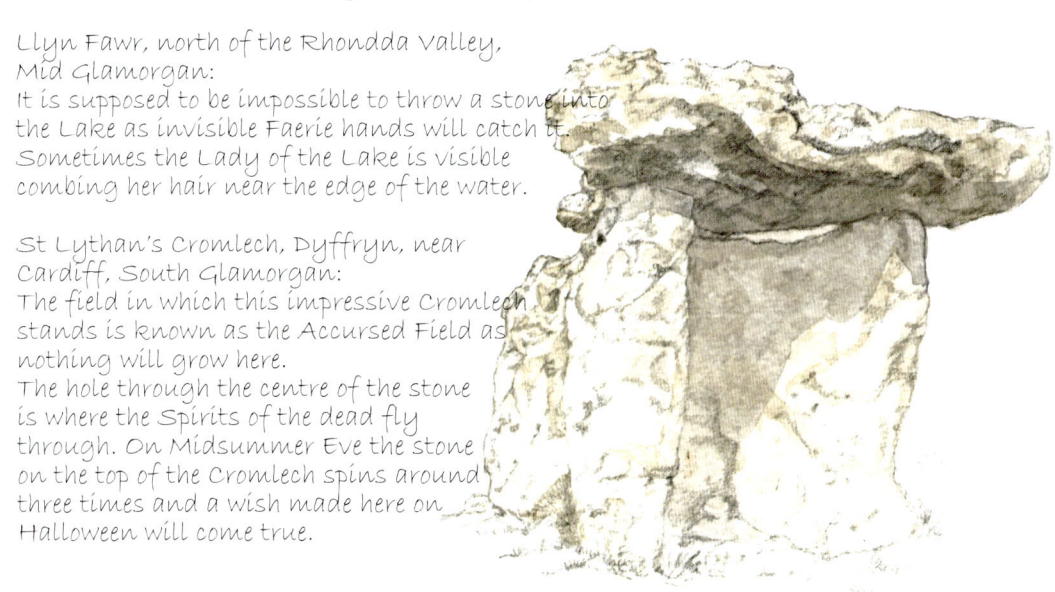

Wales

Cwm-yr Eglwys, Dinas, Dyfed:
This place was once known as Yns Fach Llyfan Gawr, the little Island of Llyfan the Giant.
Not much is known of this mysterious Giant but there have been sightings of Faeries around this village.
A faerie village can sometimes be seen in the middle of the Bay just under the water.

Llyn y Fan Fach, below Bannau Sir Gaer, Carmarthen Fans, Dyfed:
This Lake contains many faeries in its bottomless waters, and is also famed for the magical properties of the water. It is said drinking the water makes the local girls beautiful and at one time the Parish did have the reputation of having the most beautiful girls in Wales.

Old Cardiganshire's 50 mile coastline is famous for its mermaids.

Nymphs live near freshwater springs and pools, keeping the water fresh and clean. For their own survival depends on the water as they are not immortal and will die if their pools dry up.

The waters that the nymphs tend are considered to be sacred and anybody bathing in the water will benefit from its healing powers.

Shropshire

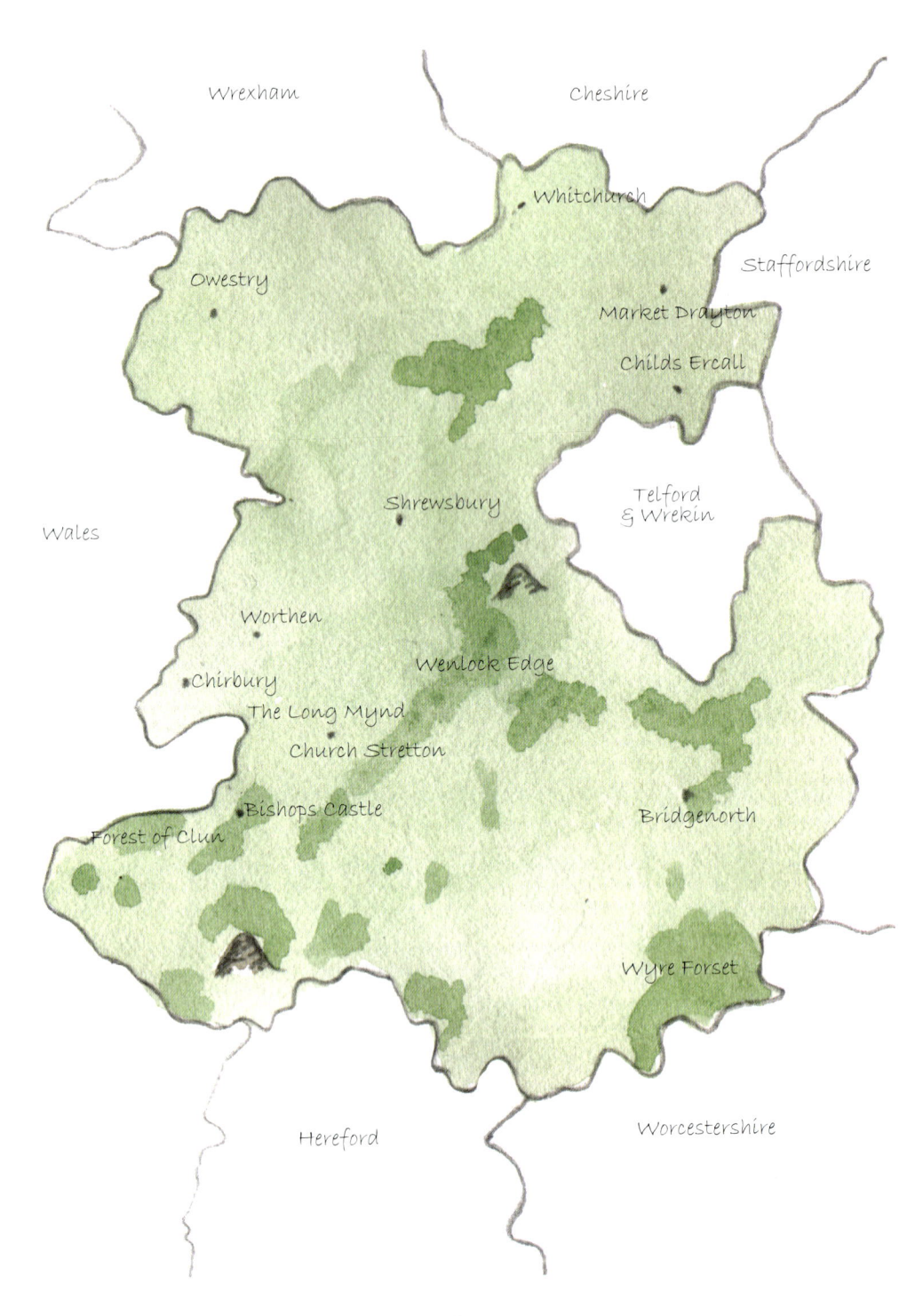

Shropshire

Worthen:
A local folktale is told of a family called Reynolds who were driven from their farm by the antics of an old man and woman Bogle.

The family packed up all their possessions and slipped away one night to another farm hoping to escape from them.

Unfortunately when they were unpacking at the new farm the wife realised she had left a precious heirloom behind in the farmhouse, so she managed to persuade Edward their cowman to return to the old farm to find it.

As he walked into the farmyard the two Bogles were waiting with the precious object in their wrinkly old hands. They refused to hand it over unless Edward promised to take them to the new farm.

The cowman made the promise and took it from them, although on the way back he did his best to lose them, the two bogles were still close behind as he got back to the new farm.

The Reynolds decided to be rid of the two Bogles once and for all, so they made Edward lie down in front of the fire and covered him with a thick layer of straw. The old man and woman Bogle were invited to sit by the fire and warm themselves, and as they sat there getting comfortable Edward emerged from the straw and thrust them into the roaring fire.

Using broom handles and pitchforks the family held the two Bogles there until they were burned to a cinder.

The Forest of Clun:
An Eleventh Century hero called Wild Eric from the Welsh Borders kidnapped a Faerie woman from the Forest. The Faerie agreed to marry him on the condition that he must never mention her Faerie Family.

Many years passed till one day after she had been missing for hours Wild Eric demanded in a rage to know whether she had been visiting her Faerie sisters. Before Wild Eric had finished speaking, she had vanished, and the heartbroken hero spent the rest of his life wandering through the Forest searching for his lost Faerie bride.

Childs Ercall:
Two farmworkers were on their way to work one morning when they saw a Mermaid rising from a local pool. She told them of the treasure that had lain at the bottom of the pool for many years and that they could take as much of it as they wished. The two men could not believe their luck so when the Mermaid dived back under the water they waded into the muddy water to follow her.

She re-emerged suddenly carrying a huge lump of Gold that was as big as the men's heads. They were so astonished that one man swore that "by God he had never had such luck in his life". Hearing his oath the Mermaid screamed and dived back into the water taking the huge lump of Gold with her. And that was the last they ever saw of the Mermaid and the treasure.

Mitchell's Fold, Chirbury:
A magical Cow once lived within this stone circle and gave an endless supply of milk to the grateful locals, who each received a pail of milk every day. Mitchell or Medgel the local witch decided that she would try to cheat the Cow by milking her into a sieve, but the Cow being a magical creature was not deceived and the witch was turned into stone for her greed.

Lincolnshire

Strangers: small creatures with arms and legs that are as thin as threads, and on the ends of these, enormous hands and feet.

They can be seen scampering about the flat lands of the Fens wearing their distinctive yellow hats in the shape of toadstools, the rest of their clothing is just the normal green jacket and breeches. Apart from this, their appearance is quite odd; they have long noses, great wide mouths out of which their tongues have a tendency to loll.

Up till quite recently, offerings were left for these people on flat stones around the Fens, the first ears of corn, and the first new potatoes of the crop. Bread and milk and also Beer would be left upon the fireplaces of the local's homes to ensure a good harvest for the following year, for the Strangers were believed to help the corn ripen and all things to grow.

The annual wages for Brownies in Lincolnshire, instead of the usual food, is the gift of a white linen smock on New Year's Eve.

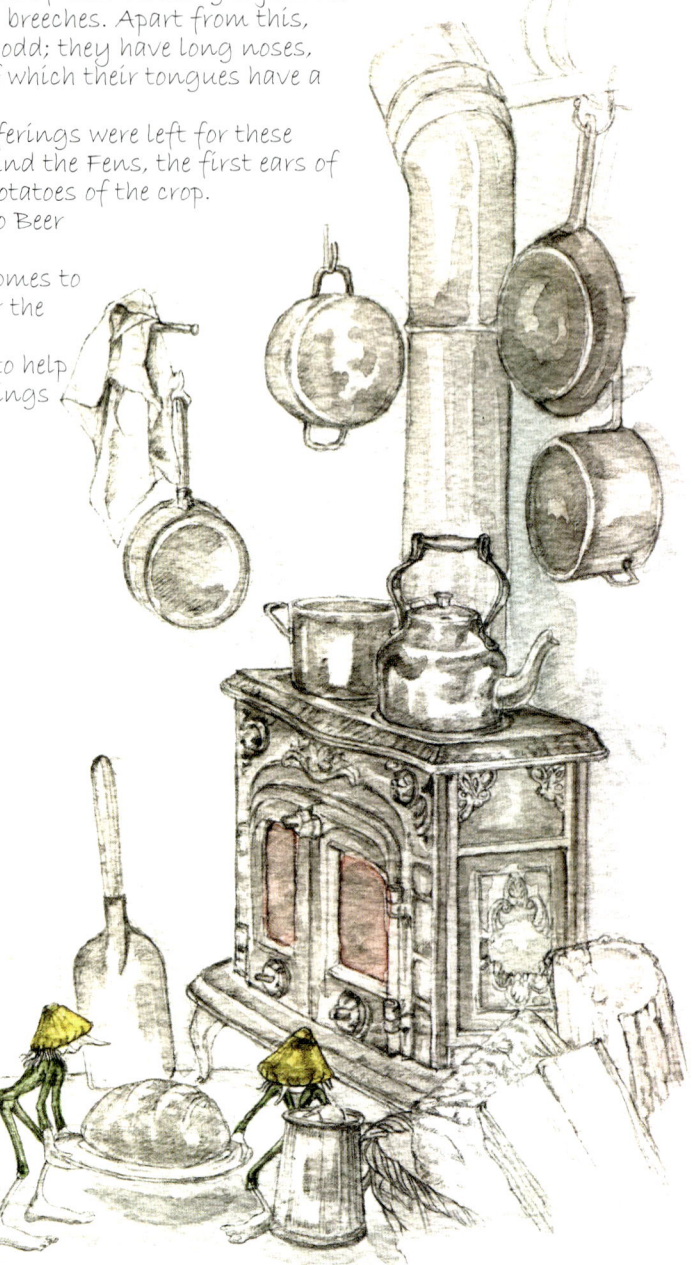

DERBYSHIRE

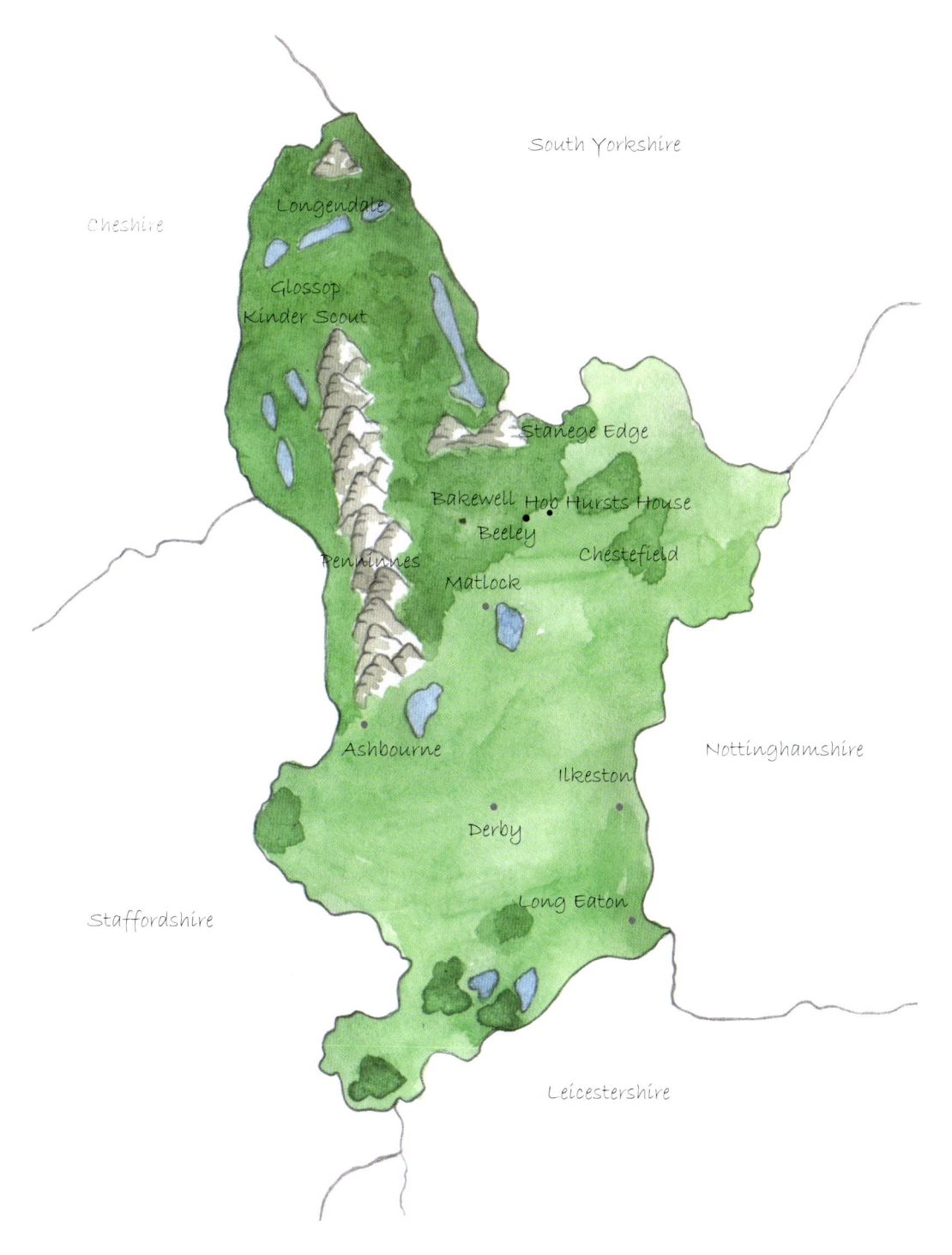

Lancashire

LANCASHIRE

Higher Penwortham: Faerie funeral processions can often be seen wending their way along the road through Penworthan Wood. If you meet this tiny procession emerging from the churchyard at midnight it is considered to be extremely unlucky.

The Black Rock: On this rock in the Mersey Estuary a Mermaid fell in love with an 18th century sailor called John Robinson. She gave the Sailor her ring just before he left on a long sea journey and she promised that they would soon be reunited. Five days later the Sailor's ship sank and all on board were drowned.

Kilmoulis: This is a Brownie that haunts Mills, although he does work for the Miller, his practical jokes can get a bit wearing. The Kilmoulis has no mouth just a very large nose, so to eat, he shoves it up his nostril.
This is all very well until he gets a cold!

Longridge: The small lanes around this place are haunted by a Boggart called the Headless Woman. From the back she looks just like a harmless old woman. Until she turns around! There is just an empty space under her hat because she carries her head in the basket on her arm.
Unlucky travellers have been chased for miles by the head which bounces down the road after them cackling and jeering.
(I wonder what the body does while the head is away?)

The Stepping stones across the River Ribble at Brungerley are haunted by a water spirit called Peg O'Nell.
Peg was a servant girl that drowned in the river hundreds of years ago. She was sent out by her Mistress one icy night to draw some water, and she slipped on the stones and fell into the river.
Peg claims a life every seven years by dragging people who are trying to cross the river into the water.

Two poachers had been raiding a rabbit warren when they heard voices coming from their bulging sacks.
"Dick wheer art ta?"
"In a sack, on a back, riding up Hoghton Brow".
The sacks were dropped pretty quickly and the two Faeries made their way back to the rabbit holes. The two poachers stayed away from that particular warren after that.

LANCASHIRE

There is a tale of the 'fetch' concerning a young man called Robin who lived in Langton.
One night the young man accompanied the local vet to a lonely farmhouse near the village; close by were the ruins of an old Priory and Church.
After dealing with the sick animal they started to make their way home through the dark when they heard the long slow strokes of a bell.
"It's the passing bell" said Robin, after two strokes, " and it's for a man" for it was the custom in those days to ring single strokes for a man, and in twos for a woman, three for a child. After a pause the strokes continued, counting the age of the dead person. Twenty-six strokes, the age of Robin himself.
The Church was dark and quiet, and as they stood there wondering who had been ringing the bell, the gate silently swung open and a strange procession entered the Churchyard.
A tiny figure led, dressed in black with just a red skull cap, chanting a dirge as he slowly paced up the path. Past the two men the tiny figures carried a coffin, and as was the custom the lid was open to allow the mourners to gaze upon the face of the deceased.
Robin and his friend, although terrified couldn't help themselves but to lean forward and gaze inside at the figure. The face was that of Robin himself.
The young man leapt forward demanding of the Faeries to know his fate but as soon as he uttered his words the procession vanished leaving the two men alone in the Churchyard.
From then on Robin was a changed man, moody and depressed he avoided all company except for his friend who had shared the ordeal in the churchyard.
One month to the day that he had seen the procession he slipped from the top of a corn stack and fell, dying shortly afterwards.
His funeral procession took the same route as that of the Faerie procession.

In the 18th and 19th Century it was the custom for brave and fearless people to venture out on New Year's Eve to wait in the local church porch.
As midnight drew nearer the spirits of those about to die in the following year from that parish would appear coming up the church path and then disappear inside .
After watching many friends, family and neighbours enter the church it was all too common for the onlooker to see himself as the last 'fetch'.

If an angry Faerie spits in your eye , you will go blind.

Green Moss taken from a mill stream, pouring salt on to the table, and saying the Lords Prayer three times is effective protection against evil Faeries.

Hobbedy's Lantern: name for the Will O the Wisp.

Padfoot: Size of a donkey, black and shaggy with fiery eyes, it follows travellers along dark lonely lanes at night. Only its soft padding footsteps can be heard behind, the creature must not be spoken to directly or even touched as this will bring bad luck.

Yorkshire

YORKSHIRE

Hobgoblins: Small, smelly and incredibly ugly but supposed to be friendly! Go prepared with a peg for your nose in case you run into one.
They are prone to playing practical jokes, so beware!

Jenny Greenteeth: Found in Yorkshire rivers, she waits in the shallows for unwary children to venture too near the river bank. If they do, a skinny arm will drag them down to a watery grave

Peg Powler is another one of the green river hags with sharp teeth that wait for children by the river banks.

Elbolton Hill, near Burnsall is well known among the locals as a Faerie residence.
One such local came across a group of Faeries dancing on the hill one moonlit night. He should have known better than to have interrupted but he got caught up in the music and called out to them offering to sing them one of his own songs. The Faeries were so cross at his interruption that they beat him black and blue. He avoided the spot from that day.

At Runswick Bay, a Hob lived in a cave called Hob Hole.
He was very popular with the locals as he had a special gift for curing whooping cough when nothing else could. The sick child would be taken to the mouth of the cave and the Hob called out too,

"Hob Hole Hob, Hob Hole Hob,
My poor bairn's gotten t'kin cough,
So tak't off!, tak't off".

And the cough would disappear within a day or two.

Pudding Pie Hill near Thirsk was made by the Faeries to live in. If you want to hear them, run around the Barrow nine times, then plunge a knife into the grass then put your ear to the ground.

Many Faeries live under hearths, they give away their presence when they steal the food left by the fire.

YORKSHIRE

Willy Howe:
This barrow close to Wold Newton is the site of many Faerie banquets. A chance passerby was once offered a drink in a beautiful goblet by one of the revellers, but he knew too well what happened to people who drank from a Faerie cup and threw the wine to the ground and ran off with the goblet.
This goblet was later said to have come into the possession of Henry the Second.

Atwick:
A spring at the bottom of the hill near the church is the home of a hobgoblin known as the Haliwell Boggle.

Boggart, also called Shriker, Barguest or Trash. Commonly takes the form of a large dog, white cow or horse and is considered to be an omen of death. He is usually blamed for the decay of wood and the collapse of wooden buildings and brings general misfortune for households and farms.
Boggarts are very seldom violent, just malicious and they like to tease. In 1825 one attacked a tradesman called Drabble and chased him around the streets until he finally made it safely back to his house.

Hazelwood and Hazelnuts give protection against Faerie bewitchment. Hazel breast bands are used on harnesses to protect the horses.

Amber, this fossilized resin has been prized since prehistoric times. It was worn as a protection against Witchcraft, poisons and the evil eye. It will also bring good luck and health to the wearer.

Jet or Black Amber has the same properties as Amber but it also used to be burnt to drive away evil spirits.

CUMBRIA

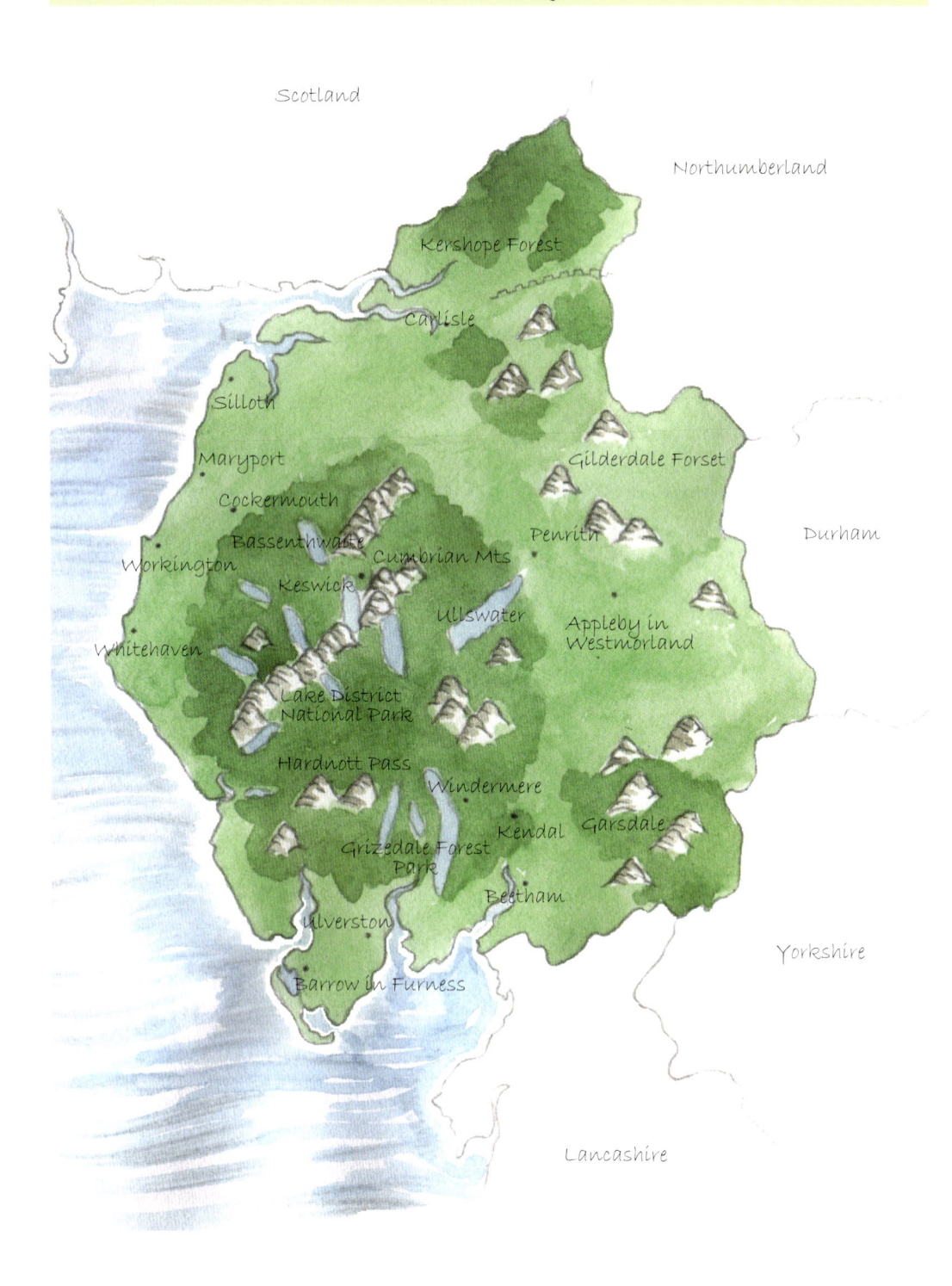

CUMBRIA

Elva Hill (North East of Bassenthwaite Lake) is a Faerie Hill. Elva meaning the place of the Elves in old Viking. The stone circle upon the hill is no longer complete, only 15 stones of the original 30 remain.

Also on the banks of Bassenthwaite Lake is Castle Howe which is the site of a Faerie Castle. On misty mornings or sometimes late in the evening the reflections of it can be seen in the waters of the Lake, but never the actual Faerie Castle.

Castle Howe.
Two children disturbed this Faerie site and roused the Faeries anger when they started digging with their toy spades.
The Father saw what they were doing and sent the dog over to attract their attention.
But before the dog could reach them, it stopped dead in its tracks as though paralysed.

CUMBRIA

Many years ago a servant from Eden Hall came upon some Faeries dancing in rings around a Green Glass Goblet.
The servant crept up on the little figures and then hurriedly snatched the Goblet. He ran all the way back to Eden Hall closely followed by the enraged Faeries; as he reached the safety of the Hall, the Faerie Queen called out to him that if ever the Goblet was broken then Eden Hall would be no more.
The Hall was demolished in 1934 but the Goblet is still unbroken and at the moment is kept in the Victoria and Albert Museum.

Hardnott Pass:
The Roman Fort of Mediobogdrm holds a Faerie festival or Rath, in amongst the ruins. Here the Faerie King holds his banquets with his vast court.

Beetham: West of the Church there are Faerie steps cut into the limestone rocks. If you can climb the steps without touching either side you will be granted a wish by the Faeries. However do not climb the stairs on the night of a full moon (it gets very busy!) as you will meet the souls of the dead descending.

There is a river in Cumbria which after flowing through several underground limestone holes, erupts during wet weather into one of the many swallow holes thereare about the area. The water looks as though its boiling thus gaining the name The Faeries Kettle.

The most famous phantom army is the one that appeared on Souther Fell in 1735. It took an hour for the vast army to march over the fell; it was seen again on the same day two years later on Midsummer's Eve.
They re-appeared on the Fell again after another two years.

DURHAM

Stanhope: The locals all know that the Weardale have more than their fair share of Faeries and that they can be anything but friendly at times. So when a local Farmer found that his young daughter had strayed into a Faerie cave, he was terrified that they would take the little girl in revenge. He quickly consulted the wise woman of the village, following her advice, he silenced everything in the house that night, the clock, the fire in case it crackled, the dogs were fed and put outside, in fact he did everything to have complete silence for when the Faeries arrived, for they cannot work their magic in silence.

At the stroke of midnight he heard them ride into the farmyard and stop, obviously puzzled by the lack of noise, until upstairs the little girl's dog started barking; the one thing that he had forgotten.

By the time he had reached her room the little girl was gone.

The next morning as soon as it was light he visited the wise woman again. The only way to get his daughter back was to give the King of the Faeries three gifts which he could not refuse and would be forced to hand back the little girl.

The three things were a real puzzle to the Farmer, he did not know what they meant or how to get them. Something that gave light without burning, a live chicken without a bone in its body and he had to collect a limb from a living animal without spilling any blood.

The farmer walked slowly home trying to work out this riddle when he was distracted by a commotion in the trees, a kestrel had hold of a lizard by the tail, which promptly shed it and disappeared into the grass. So he had one of the gifts and by the time he had got home he had worked out another part of the riddle; one of his hens had been sitting on a clutch of eggs for 15 days and he knew that although alive the chick's bones would not yet have formed. So now he had two gifts safely collected. As for the third he puzzled all day until the night began to draw in, so he made up his mind to go to the cave and hope that he would find the third gift on the way. It was quite dark by the time that he reached the hills and he could clearly see a green glow in the grass. A glow worm was the third gift. The farmer called to the Faerie King to release his daughter and as he was just about to refuse, the three gifts were laid in front of him, the Faeries disappeared and the little girl came running out of the cave.

After that she stayed close to home, knowing better than to meddle with the Faeries that live in the Dale.

Puck also known as Robin Goodfellow.
He is able to change his shape at will using this ability for mischief to trick people. Often portrayed with goat's legs and horns. He appears in Shakespeare's 'A midsummer night's dream'.

If you have a house Brownie or Sprite that is making a nuisance of itself try scattering millet seed on the floor every night. It will soon get fed up with clearing it up and leave.

Brown Man of the Muirs is the guardian of all the wild animals and birds on Elsden Moors.
He is devoted to all his animals and takes a rather nasty revenge on anybody who harms one.

NORTHUMBERLAND

NORTHUMBERLAND

Hedley On The Hill:
The Hedley Kow is a Bogle who makes a nuisance of himself by putting machinery out of order, knocking over cooking pots and unravelling knitting.

Hylton Castle used to be the home of a Brownie called The Cauld Lad. Like most Brownies he was happiest when he was busy tidying and cleaning up. Unfortunately he had a rather annoying habit of making work for himself by unmaking beds, emptying cupboards and throwing things around the rooms of the Castle. The other servants became tired of his antics and decided they would encourage the Brownie to leave the Castle. The traditional method for doing this would be to give the Brownie a set of new clothes to wear. So the servants laid out a smart new cloak and hood for him, and it worked, the Cauld Lad took offence immediately and left the Castle for ever. Of course the servants had twice as much work to do once the Brownie had left, but that serves them right for being so mean!

Rothley: On the banks of the Hart Burn are several rocks with small holes in them, this is where the Faeries cool their porridge, which they make in the nearby Mill. Taking oats from the sacks and cooking it in the Miller's own cooking pot!
Many years ago a previous Mill owner became very annoyed at his oats disappearing in this way, so he waited until the Faeries had crept into the building and were busy bending over the cooking pot, he then dropped a stone down the chimney. The Miller was hoping to frighten away the Faeries but unluckily for him the stone dropped into the boiling porridge, and the hot oats splashed out and scalded the gathered Faeries.
Screaming in anger the Faeries rushed out of the Mill to find the culprit and there scrambling down from the roof was the Miller. They chased him for miles down the river bank. Records do not show whether he was caught by the angry Faeries but subsequent owners have never interrupted the nightly cooking of the porridge again.

There lived at Rothley a very clever little boy that once outwitted a Faerie girl. One night despite his mothers warning that the Faeries would get him if he didn't go to bed, he stayed up alone playing in front of the fire. Down the chimney flew a beautiful little Faerie girl and joined in the boy's game.
Ainsel was her name she informed the boy and he, being rather quick and cheeky, said he was My ainsel.
They stayed playing together until the fire began to die down, the little boy stretched, and rose to stir the fire with a poker. One of the embers fell on the Faerie's foot and as she screeched out that she was burnt, a voice echoed down the chimney asking who had burnt her daughter's foot. With a cloud of soot the Faerie's mother stood before the little boy asking again who had burnt her foot.
"My ainsel, My ainsel" she crowed, delighted that she would get the little boy into trouble.
"Then in that case" said the Mother "What's all the fuss about?". And shooed her daughter back up the chimney.

IRELAND

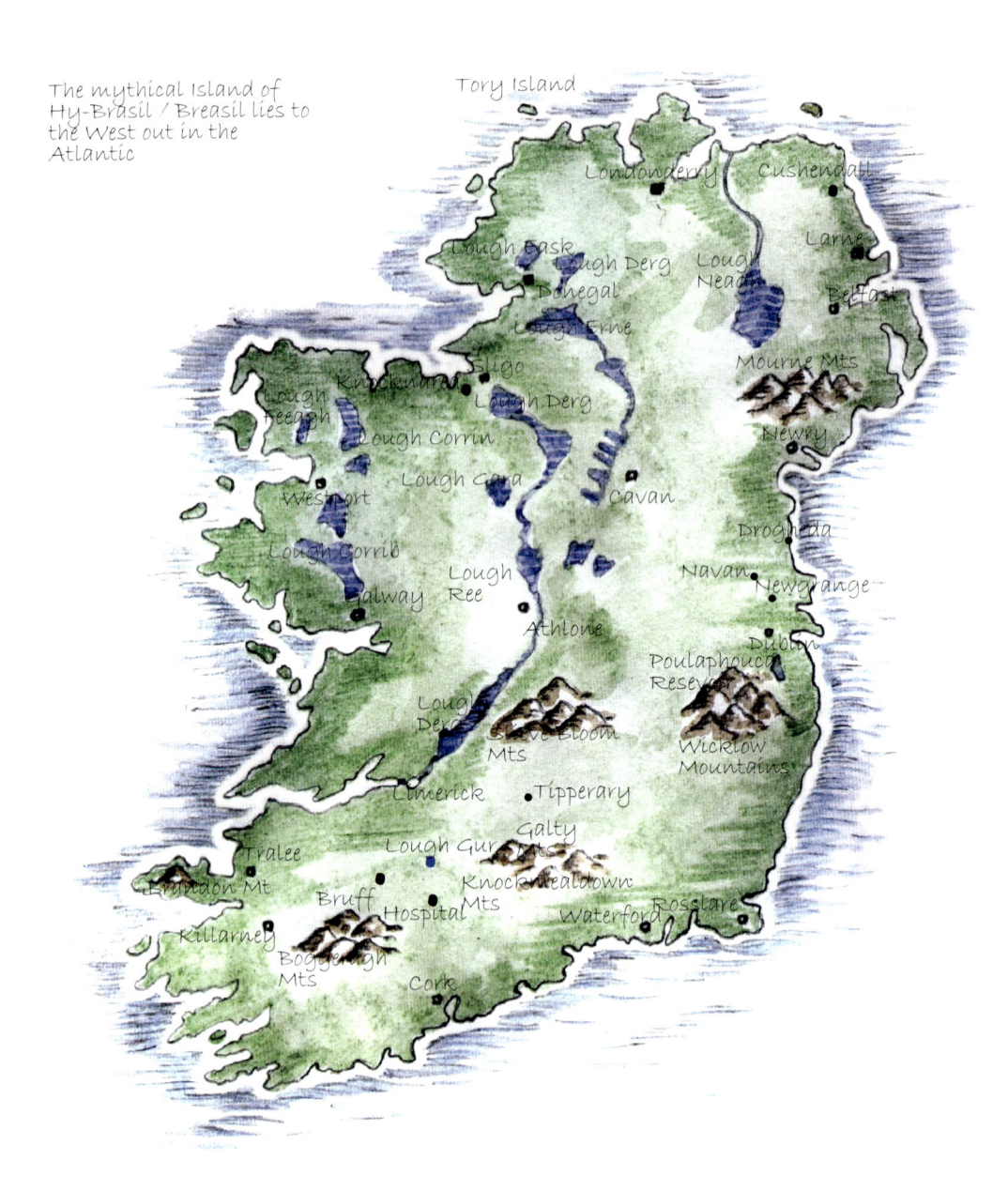

The mythical Island of Hy-Brasil / Breasil lies to the West out in the Atlantic

IRELAND

Leprechaun: The Fairy Shoemaker who wears a red cap.
Usually lives around pure streams and haunts cellars. Spends his time drinking and smoking.
Each Leprechaun possesses a crock of Gold, if caught by a mortal he will promise to reveal the location of the Gold.
But if the mortal takes his eyes off him even to blink the Leprechaun will vanish.

One way to distract him is to admire his skill in making shoes and then make off with the gold.

Another way to find the Leprechaun's gold is to locate the end of a rainbow, if you can do this it will pinpoint the exact location.

The Leprechaun wears two leather purses in each of which is a silver and gold coin.
The silver coin returns magically to his purse even after being given away.
The gold coin is only given away when the Leprechaun needs to buy his freedom, and while the human is busy congratulating himself and examining the coin the Leprechaun will disappear and the coin will turn to ashes.

IRELAND

Good People: the Irish often referred to their Sidhe in this way.

People of Peace, the Sidhe are called this as Sidhe means Peace

An excavation in 1938 of the Giants Grave near Lough Gur raised the wrath of the Banshees. A great wailing was heard around the district for many days until they had replaced the dead where they belonged.

Merrows: These are the Irish merpeople and can be told apart from the others by the red feathered caps that they wear. These caps are used to propel themselves down to their homes in the depths of the sea, if these are lost then they cannot return home.
The female Merrows are very beautiful and gentle even though they appear before storms as an omen.
They sometimes fall in love with mortal fishermen which is quite understandable as the male Merrows are extremely ugly, although they are jovial in nature.

A cloud is sometimes seen around the Lough and the older locals know that the Dead Hunt is out, their quarry is the souls of people about to die.

A cave on the Island of Knockadoon in the middle of the Lough is one of the many entrances to Ti'r Na n' O'g 'The Land Of Eternal Youth'

There are other entrances in Lough Corrib and Lough Neagh.

IRELAND

Tuatha de Danann: (meaning children of the Goddess Danu) They are the most important race of Faeries in Ireland.
They were wafted into Ireland on a magical cloud and set down in Western Connaught.
The Danann brought with them from over the sea four magical gifts,
1. The Stone of Destiny.
2. The Sword of Lugh of the Long Arm, this was supposed to make the bearer invincible.
3. A Magic Spear.
4. The Cauldron of Dagda, which had the ability to feed hordes of people without ever becoming empty.

The King of the Dananns was Nuadu. When they fought against the Fir Bolg, Nuadu lost a hand in the battle, which was replaced by a silver one.
He was then known as Nuadu Airgetlam, Nuadu of the Silver Hand.
He was later killed during the Dananns conflict with the Formorians.
After that the Tuatha de Dananns were driven deep into the mountains and the otherworld by the invading Milesians.

The home of the Dananns could be reached through the gateway of the ancient burial chambers of Kilclooney More Tomb near Nairn Co. Donegal.

The horses of the Tuatha are urivalled even by the Scottish Kelpies for their speed and endurance but they are so fierce that they cannot be tamed by any mortal.

An annual battle would take place between the Faeries of Cnoc 'Aine and those of Cnoc Firinne; they would hold a cross country hurling match the length and breadth of Ireland.
And the prize ?
A bag of potatoes!

Humans would also be drafted in to take part in these games, as well as the fights that would break out from time to time between the different Faerie tribes.

Any new building must be passed first with the Faerie Planners (in case the building crosses a Faerie Path) Four piles of stones are placed at the corners of the site, if the stones are still there in the morning it is ok to go ahead with the building.
If this is not done the owner of the new building will have broken furniture and crockery, sick animals and sometimes the Faeries can take even worse revenge.

The three leafed clover as well as being the emblem of Ireland is an ancient sacred symbol.
It has strong associations with the Sun and is worshipped by the Tuatha de Danaan, symbolising the spring equinox.

IRELAND

The Mound of Hostages, Tara

Tara, Navan, County Meath.
This is an ancient burial site famous as the capital of the high Kings of Ireland and a holy site for thousands of years.
Originally named Temair after a Princess Tea married an Irish King.
The Princess brought with her as a gift to the high Kings the Tuatha de Danann's legendary Stone of Destiny, the Lia-Fail.
Much spiritual power and strength dwells in this stone and it is on this that the King would sit at his coronation.
If he is the rightful heir the stone roars beneath him.
It was removed from Tara by Prince Fergus and taken to Iona, from there the Scottish King Kenneth MacAlpine carried it off to Scone.
But that was not the end of its travels; Edward the First then had it carried to Westminster Abbey in 1296 and built into the throne used for English Coronations.
Near the centre of the main part of the site is the Fort of the Kings and on top of the high mound stands a stone which is called the Lia-Fail although this is not the original stone of the Tuatha de Dananns.

Daniel O Donoghue is the King of the Faeries in Connaught.

The Cluricaun is a male Faerie that is closely related to the Leprechaun, he is found in the cellars of Inns where he'll protect the wine and kegs of Beer in exchange for a few drinks. He can cause trouble if denied his payment but usually brings good luck to the Inn.

IRELAND

Pookas: Irish Goblin which haunts the Irish Lakes, they usually take the form of a large black dog or a horse.
Similar to the kelpie it also appears to be friendly until it has persuaded you to mount, then it will take you on a wild ride across the Irish countryside before dumping you into a bog. Many places in Ireland are named after the Pooka, Lissapuca, Rathpuca and Poulapuca or Pooka's Pool in Wicklow.
A Mr. Martin from Dublin claimed to have seen the Derry Pooka while on a fishing holiday in 1928.

Some describe the Phookas of Ireland as ghosts, trapped because of their laziness in the mortal world. One is supposed to be a spirit of a lazy kitchen boy who has to perform countless chores in the shape of a Donkey, once it is deemed that he has worked hard enough he will be set free.

The Gentry: The most noble tribe of all the Faeries in Ireland, a large race that came from the planets. They usually appear in white; the locals make sure that they bless The Gentry frequently to protect themselves from harm.

Fir Darrig: (fear dead) related to the leprechaun. Delights in playing unpleasant practical jokes. Treat with care.

Lunantishness: These are the tribes that guard the sloe and blackthorn trees in Ireland. They will let no one to cut a branch or damage the tree on the eleventh of November or the eleventh of May which was the original May day.

The hill at Cnoc'Aine, Co Limerick, has been the setting for many torch lit revels by the faerie followers of the Goddess 'Aine.

In Munster, Lough Gur is well known to be an enchanted place, even to fall asleep on its banks in the daytime is a very dangerous thing to do.

Aine is often seen lying in the water in the form of a mermaid combing her hair.

Every seven years the waters of the loch drain away to reveal the magical tree of life that grows under the waters.

Faerie thorns: Not even dead branches lying under the tree should be taken away. If a branch is broken by accident it should be tied back into position.
It is very unlucky to destroy a sacred tree. It will release harmful spirits which are bound within the tree and would give bad luck to the surrounding people.
If the tree is destroyed then a new one must be planted in the same position.

The well known Irish walking stick the shillelagh is made from Blackthorn but it must not be cut from a living tree on the 11th November as this is the day of the Dead, neither on the 11th of May.

IRELAND

Dublachan: Dark creatures that appear where a violent death is about to take place. For some reason they are more prevalent in Sligo.

Tash or Thershi appears in either animal or human form, they are the spirit of somebody who has suffered a violent death and they are bound to haunt the place of that death as a lesson to others.

Leanhaun Shee: The Faerie Mistress. She is so beautiful that all men fall in love with her. She inspires musicians and poets which all die young; she will not allow them to practice their arts long in the mortal world.
Once a man is ensnared, his life force is slowly sucked away, the only escape is if another man will take his place.

Fear Garta: The Man of Hunger, a rather nasty creature that pops up during times of famine. In more fruitful times he remains hidden within the ground.
He can be appeased with offerings of food.

A Faerie Rade of mortal size is led by King Finvarra who ruled over the Faeries of Western Ireland, and who also known as the King of the Dead and his Queen Oonagh. Their troupe of followers is made up of the recent and ancient dead and any mortal who sees them on Halloween will be captured and will have to ride with them for ever. Finvarra was the most well known of Ireland's Faerie Kings, his wife Oonagh was also renowned for her beauty.
But for all her beauty Finvarra was obsessed with mortal women, spiriting them away to Faerieland. They would be returned later to the mortal world, complete with a Faerie pregnancy.
He also was said to have a second wife called Nuala, and in his spare time he was fond of hurling and chess.

Metal breaks harmful magic and noise drives away demons.

The evil spirits that come to the bedside of the dead and dying are kept at bay by the ringing of the passing bell.

IRELAND

Picts: The original people who lived on the northeastern coast. Called the Cruithne they were originally from Gaul or France. They eventually retreated to the woods and lived in caves and underground forts.

Daoine Sidhe: They live in underground Palaces of Gold and crystal and are blessed with youth, beauty, joy and great musical ability.
The word Sidh means an enchanted mound dwelling, and the Sidhe have homes in the many Tumuli scattered over Ireland such as New Grange.

New Grange Passage Tomb, Brugh Na Boinne, Meath.
This is one of the finest passage graves in Ireland and it is situated in the ancient Boyne Valley Cemetery.
There are three great mounds, three chambers within, a 62 ft passage leads to one chamber. The walls are huge slabs, all carved with intricate spiral and geometric patterns.

Offerings of Gold, Jewellery and coins were buried at New Grange for the Faeries.
It was believed that they were the guardians of the land and the health and fertility of animals and crops depended upon their cooperation.

IRELAND

Firbolgs: People of the Bogs (or Bags). They were a race of beings who invaded Ireland from Europe, later banished from Ireland by the Tuatha de Danann

Formorians:: One of the original invading groups, their stronghold was on Tory Island off the coast of Donegal. They were a savage people but were also defeated by the Tuatha da Danann. They were driven into the sea where they changed into sea demons although they are able to travel on land if they leave the sea at night.

Knocknarea, Sligo:
On the top of the 1000 ft Knocknarea Mountain is the huge cairn known as Mosgaun Meabha; this is the burial place of Queen Mab. The cairn is 200 ft in diameter and 34 ft high.

Bean Tighe: She is the Irish form of the Faerie Godmother, she will attach herself to certain families for many generations, looking after the children and pets, even finishing the chores around the house.

Fear Dearc: This 2 ½ foot high man can be found in Munster, is usually quite visible in a red sugar loaf hat, long red coat, grey straggly hair and wrinkled face.
He visits many of the farms in the area, warming himself by the fires, nobody objects as he brings good luck to the farm.

Gancener: A pipe smoking Faerie who appears to young girls in lonely places. He is obviously very charming as all the young girls pine away and die for the love of him.

Ballybog: A small brown Faerie who lives in the peat bogs, they are given offerings in return for peat for the villagers fires.

When St Patrick visited Ireland, he was insulted by some local women, and he took his revenge by turning them all into fish. After a while he relented and turned them into underwater Sea Faeries instead.

IRELAND

Bean Sidhe: This is the Irish Banshee; she will wail before the death of members of certain families. Also called the White Lady of Sorrow. Usually seen wearing a long grey cloak with a veil, with eyes red from weeping.
If several of these Banshees wail together then it means that someone great or very holy has just died. Some Irish funeral music is said to have been based on the Banshee's wailing which is supposed to be quite beautiful.

Bean Fionn: A white robed woman who will drag children and travellers to their deaths in the rivers of Ireland.

Footprints contain the essence of a person and by using spells and charms combined with the dust and dirt from it, power can be obtained over that person.

If you come in contact with Faeries on All Hallows Eve (Halloween) make sure you throw some dirt from your own footprint after the Faeries, this will protect you and any mortals that the Faeries have stolen away will be surrendered as well.

Brass and Iron are effective in repelling evil spirits, it can also be worn as a fertility charms.

Isle of Man

ISLE OF MAN

Cabbyl Ushtey: A Water horse, similar to a Kelpie and it shares its nasty habit of dunking riders. Can be spotted by its back to front hooves.

Tarroo Ushtey: Very ferocious water bull, it haunts the coastal waters and rivers.

Fairy cattle can be seen at dawn standing in the meadows. They have white bodies, red eyes and ears. There are also Faerie pigs with large frilly ears and tails.

The Manx Fenoderee: Banished from the Ferishey, the small group of Manx Trouping Faeires, the Fenoderee was deprived of his beauty because he missed the Autumn Equinox Festival to dance with a mortal girl in the Glen of Rushen. He was condemned to wear a hairy, ugly form until the day of Judgement.

The Fenoderee has been known to help the islanders, in one case he moved some large stones for the building of a house at Snafield. They had been too heavy for the builders and had been left at the quarry while the men worked out how to move them.
The owner had been so grateful for the Fenoderee's help that he had a special set of clothes made just for him and laid them where the Fenoderee could find them.
"Cap for the head, alas poor head!
Coat for the back, alas poor back!
Breeches for the breech, alas poor breech!
If all these things be mine, mine cannot be the merry Glen of Rushen!"

He said this frowning sadly and then disappeared.

It is possible to call him back with special incantations and charms but caution is needed as he can be malicious at times.

Shan Cashtal, Andreas:
Faeries travel undergound from this prehistoric earthworks to Maughhold Church where they emerge into the cemetery.

The Isle of Man takes its name from the Irish sea god Manannan Mac Lir, He was the first King of the Island and had many magical powers.
He was a shape shifter, possessed a boat that obeyed his thoughts and an amazing sword that no armour was strong enough to withstand.
The King's chariot was drawn by huge horses that took the form of waves. Now any wild storm that crashes against the shoreline of the Island is believed to be the old King returning to his Kingdom.

The Faeries on the Island are well known to be keen huntsmen and are seen many times dashing over the hills in pursuit of invisible game.
One such occasion a Sailor was returning from a long voyage and was on his way to visit his Sister who lived at Kirk - Merlugh. As he drew near to the the hill between Douglas and Kirk -Merlugh he heard the sound of horns and baying hounds. There in the distance he could see the hunting party all dressed in green and riding fine white horses, The party swept passed him and although he tried to keep up with them they soon disappeared from sight.

Isle of Man

The Glashans: A type of Brownie who never wears clothes and has a habit of stealing women. But they can be useful about the farms in return for food.

Buggane: A nasty little Goblin which can change shape and size when it likes. A black Bull or a huge Ram is its favourite shape.
They haunt old chapels to hinder any attempt of repair.
St Trinian's near Greeba Mountain has been roofless for many years due to the intervention of a Buggane.

Faerie Hill, Orrisdale, Kirk Malew.
Faeries meet at this Barrow to hold feasts, during these gatherings a magical potion is passed around in a Silver Goblet.
A traveller came across one such gathering and was spotted by the Faeries as he lurked in the shadows. They called the mortal over to the gathering and offered him a drink from the silver goblet, the man took the cup in his hand but he knew too well what happened to humans foolish enough to drink from a faerie cup, so he threw the magic potion to the ground. Everything went dark, the Faeries and their banquet disappeared, leaving the man clutching the goblet.
It was later presented to the church of Kirk Malew to be used as a communion cup, but the Faerie powers still lingered within the cup and anybody drinking from it went mad shortly afterwards.

The thick mists that cover the Island from time to time is the result of a Mermaid's curse.
Her romantic advances to a local Fisherman were rejected and out of spite she placed the curse on the whole Island

The locals have a custom of leaving water out for the Faeries. If this is not done they will drink the blood of the occupants of the house when they are sleeping, or they will bleed them and make a cake with the blood.
The Faeries will leave a piece of this cake hidden in the house to bind the spell. This must be found, and fed to the sleepers or they will die of the sleeping sickness.

Few Islanders will cross Ballana Bridge on the Douglas to Castletown Road without giving a polite greeting to the Faeries that live beneath it.

A spirit lives in Nikkesens Pool in Glen Roy and emerges every now and then disguised as a handsome young man. He will then woo the local young girls and take the lovestruck young girls back to his pool, where of course they are never seen again!.

Isle of Man

The Fairy Saddle, Braddon:
Long ago a vicar of Braddon was mystified by the state of his horse every morning, although the beast had been in its field all night, it would be sweating and exhausted when the vicar would go to fetch it.
The mystery was solved when early one morning the vicar saw a small man wearing a green riding jacket returning the horse to its field. On seeing the vicar the little man vanished leaving the saddle propped up against the field's stone wall.
The saddle turned to stone and was placed on the wall by the angry vicar to discourage any other Faeries borrowing the horse.

Phynnodderee: A strong long armed Goblin who is very stupid but can be useful.
A helpful Phynnodderee offered to help a Shepherd bring in his flock of sheep from the hills. Much later the Goblin trailed in exhausted, complaining that the Shepherd's small brown sheep had caused him endless trouble when he was trying to round it up with the others.
The Shepherd was very puzzled when he heard this, all his flock were snowy white. So he went to inspect the sheep and cowering in the middle of the flock was an exhausted small brown hare.

Any mother on the Isle of Man taking her child to its christening would carry a piece of bread and cheese and give it to the first person she would meet. This was supposed to protect it from the Faeries.

Also placing salt under a milk churn and throwing stale water over a plough would be effective against the child being stolen.

To protect livestock a cross of twigs would be tied to a cow's tail.
Picking wildflowers and bringing them into the house would protect the home.

Sleigh Beggey (sleigh beargar):
The little folk, a name used for the Faeries in the Manx tongue.

Howlaa Manx: A spirit that wails on the shore before a storm.

The Manx Faeries are also known as Lil 'Fellas, the Crowd, the Mob, and themselves.

Shoopi Hee: This is a sea horse or Kelpie.

FAERIE GLAMOUR

The Faeries art of concealing their true appearance is called Glamour and is often used to deceive mortals. They can alter their own shape as well as the appearance of food, money and surroundings. So a splendid feast spread out on a beautiful gold table could be nothing more that nuts and berries laid on a log.
The use of Faerie ointment on your eyes will allow you to see them in their true state but be careful the Faeries do not find out as their wrath can be terrible and the user will be blinded.

The term Glamour comes from the Scottish word glaumerie which means magic, traditionally this power was used to capture mortal partners for breeding. As mentioned before the Faeries are always trying to improve their own race by mingling it with human blood.
To guard against this it is customary for Brides to be surrounded by bridesmaids similarly dressed so the Faerie would be confused when trying to seize the Bride. This also applied to the Groom, as the Wedding night is considered to be the most powerful time for mating with Faerie kind. The Bride or Groom might be returned later but as time in Faerie land is different to the mortal world their family and friends would be old or dead.

FAERIE GLAMOUR

The story of Eilian of Garth Darwen illustrates the power of Faerie glamour very well. Eilian was a poor servant girl who worked long hard hours for a local midwife. When one day she disappeared it was agreed by her mistress and those about her that Eilian had gone off with the Faeries. The servant girl was not seen for some time until the Midwife was called out one stormy night by a stranger to attend his wife, who was about to give birth.

She was taken to a fine looking house and inside to a richly furnished room where a woman lay on a bed. After a while the Baby was delivered and the Father asked the Midwife to rub an ointment onto the baby's eyes, this she did but also accidentally smeared some onto one of her own eyes.

Instantly the beautiful room disappeared and instead there was just a damp dark cave and on a bed of bracken and dry grass lay the servant girl Eilian.

The Midwife was seemingly paid well with gold coins but by the time she had hurried home they had disappeared and just dried leaves lay in her purse.

Several months passed before she saw the father again, strolling through the market place. He was very surprised that the midwife could see him to enquire after Eilian and the baby. He inquired with which eye did the midwife see him with and when he discovered which one, that eye went blind.

SCOTLAND

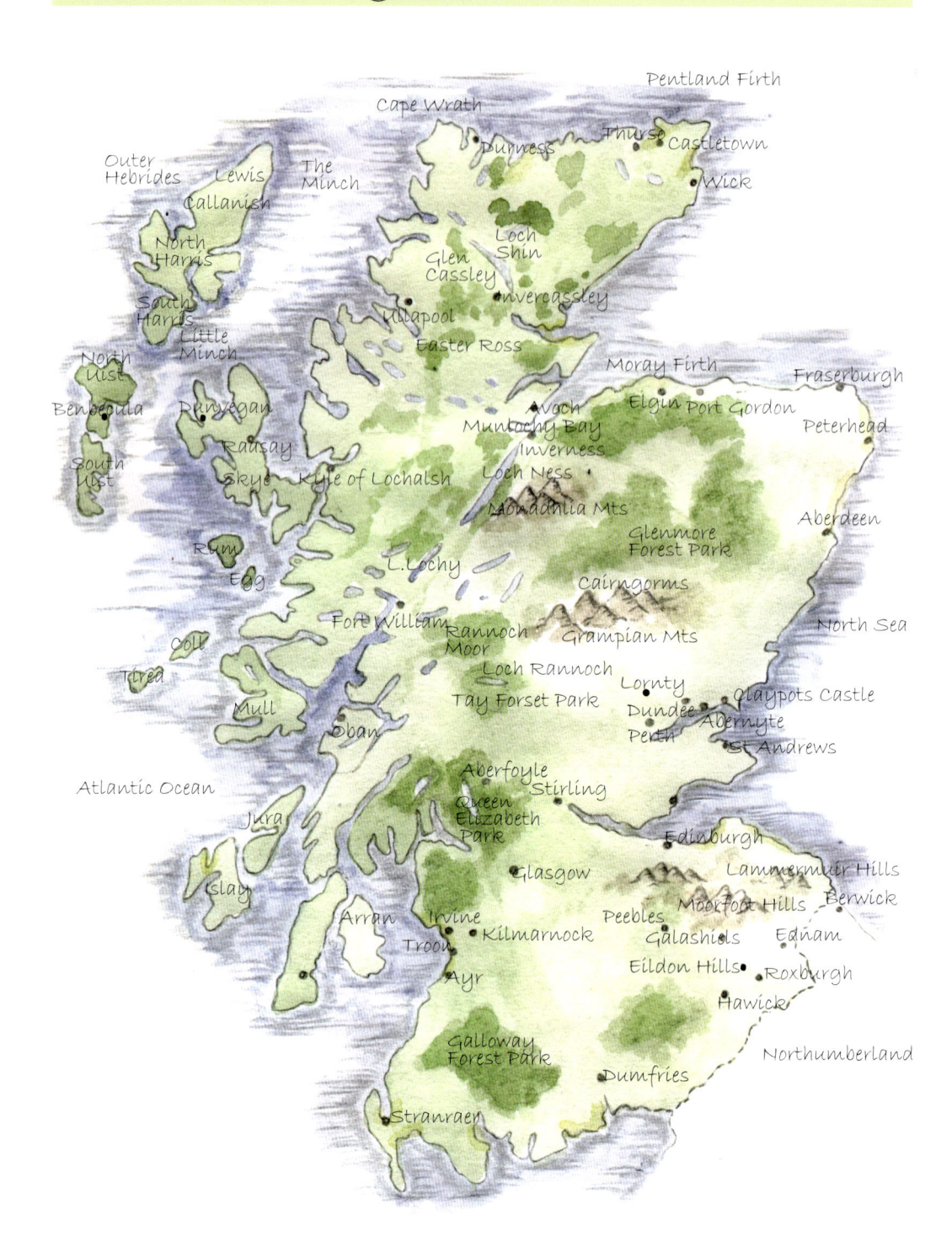

Scotland

Selkies: Shape shifting sea Faeries usually in the form of a bright eyed seal, found in Northern Scotland and the Shetland Isles. They often come on land in human form where they will dance under the light of the full moon.
When they take their human form they have to shed their seal skins. They have to hide them very carefully for without them they are unable to return to the sea. The Selkies can be told apart from humans because they still have webbed fingers and toes when on land.

There are many stories of the local Clans taking Selkie wives by stealing their skins. The women make good wives but always long for the sea so if they can recover their skins they will disappear back to the sea.

The waters around Scotland are teeming with Mermaids as well, and there have been many sightings through the years.

A Merman is often seen in the waters around Portgordon. The local Fishermen are never pleased to see him as they regard him as an evil omen. If they spot him while out fishing they will head back to the safety of the harbour.
In a report sent to the Aberdeen Chronicle in 1814 he was described as being of a tawny colour with a swarthy countenance, his green hair was quite short and curled and he had small eyes, a flat nose and a large mouth.

A Scottish Mermaid fell in love with a local Fisherman and to win his love gave him many gifts of gold and jewels.
Then unfortunately she found out that he had been giving her presents to a local girl in the village that he had been courting.
The Mermaid was determined not to share her sweetheart with anybody else, so she persuaded the Fisherman to follow her to a cave under Darwick Head near Castletown. There piled inside was all the treasure she had collected from the many shipwrecks in the Pentland Firth. The man stood there astounded at all the wealth in the cave, while he stood there mesmerised, the Mermaid began to sing low and soft.
The Fisherman's eyes grew heavy and he fell into a deep sleep. When he awoke he found himself fixed to the walls with golden chains, and if all accounts are true he is there still, keeping his jealous sweetheart company.

The Mac Codrum Clan from North Uist are descended from such a mixed marriage. They are known as Sliochd Nan Ron, the offspring of the Seals. Their ancestor took her skin while she danced in the moonlight and kept it hidden for many years, during that time they had lots of children together. There are many different explanations for the origins of Selkies, one that they are fallen angels like the Faeries and are condemned to stay like seals until the day of judgement, or that they used to be mortal but after committing some dreadful crime were punished by having to wear a seal skin for the rest of their life.
There is even one legend that says that the Selkies are the souls of drowned Sailors, and that they are allowed to return to land one night of the year to visit their families.
In the islands of Scotland the children of these marriages would often have webbing between fingers and toes. This would be clipped off by the mothers but the more it would be removed the scalier the skin would become. Anybody on the islands with hard scaly skin on their hands is undoubtedly a descendant from a Selkie.

SCOTLAND

Newark Bay, Deerness,
A mermaid was a regular visitor to this Bay, seen on many occasions by the hundreds of visitors to the area.
The reports suggest that she was an extremely large Mermaid, six to seven feet in length. She was often seen quite clearly, as a rock in the bay was her favourite place to sit.

In 1913 another Mermaid was seen sunning herself on the rocks off the coast of Hoy.
She was spotted by the crew of a fishing boat.
The reports suggested that she had been wearing some kind of shiny material wrapped around the upper part of her body, which is very unusual for a Mermaid.
She was only seen a few times after that.

As mentioned before on Page 13 it is the desire for Mermaids to marry mortal men but in Scotland it is believed that if they do not manage this and have to marry Mermen instead, the beautiful Mermaid will become uglier and uglier and end up looking like their mothers.
(This is something a lot of mortal men will sympathise with).

One family living in Easter Ross in the Hebrides have a Merman as an ancestor way back in the 19th Century,
He had lost his magic Belt and so could not return to the sea.

The Clan McVeagh in the Sutherland district also say they are descended from a marriage between a mermaid and a fisherman

Mill Bay, Stronsay:
There is a pile of rocks here called the Mermaids Chair. This rock was frequented by a Mermaid who would sit here at night singing to the stormy seas.

About 1830 a Mermaid's body was washed up on the shore at Benqula.
She had been spotted earlier in the week by men cutting seaweed and was believed to have been mortally wounded by boys throwing stones.
She was about the size of a three or four year old child with abnormally developed breasts. She had long dark hair and the lower part of her body resembled a Salmon but without the scales. Crowds of locals turned up to view the body before the body was placed wrapped in a shroud into the coffin. Her
grave is somewhere above the high water mark.

SCOTLAND

Hundreds of years ago a huge worm made its home in the slopes of the valley of Cassley in Sutherland, Scotland.
This fierce gigantic worm laid waste to the entire valley and surrounding countryside with her poisonous breath. The crofters and their families had to leave their homes and the valley was soon deserted except for the giant worm. It would crawl out from its lair at sunset and coil itself round the hill of Cnoc na Cnoimh and gloat over the destruction of the valley. The King of Scotland offered a huge reward to any man who could slay the giant worm; many brave men tried but they all failed until a farmer, Hector Gunn from the valley, stepped forward. Nobody believed that he could succeed where so many brave men had failed but Hector was a brave man and he had faith in himself. He made his way to the lair but the worm's poisonous breath drove him back. Undaunted he rode up onto the moor and cut himself a large clod of peat. Cutting the longest stick that he could find in a thicket, he thrust the peat onto the end and placed it into the fire. Hector waited until the peat was smouldering well then mounted his horse and galloped back to the valley. The sun was setting as he got there and the worm had emerged and was lazily coiling itself around the hill. As he drew nearer, the giant worm opened its huge mouth and breathed out its poisonous breath. Hector held his breath and plunged the burning clod of peat straight down the worm's throat. The worm writhed in agony as the peat burnt its soft gullet, its coils wrapped tighter and tighter around the hill.
Hector leapt from his horse and with his sword chopped off the worm's head. This he carried back in triumph to the King of Scotland to claim his reward.
The people of Cassley Valley all returned home but they always had a reminder of the worm for it had left deep spiral grooves around the hill of Cnoc na Cnoimh in its death throes; which can still be seen now.

The Nuckalavee X is the most awful water spirit that you could see. It is a Scottish sea faerie that shows itself as a huge horse with legs that are part flipper, a huge mouth and one fiery eye. Rising from its back there is a torso with long arms that reach to the ground, topped by a huge head. It has no skin and its muscles and veins are clearly visible. If you are unlucky enough to encounter this beauty just remember that it has an aversion to running water so you have to find a river or stream pretty smartish!.

"Good Neighbours"

Klippe, the Forfarshire name for fairy.
"Still Folk"
"Wee Folk"

Orkneys:
A pregnant mother would take great care to conceal her condition to avoid the attention of the Faeries and Trows.
After the birth of the baby, the cradle would be rocked day and night to stop the child from being stolen.

Cailleach Bheur is the Blue Hag of the Highlands. She takes the form of an old woman and is usually dressed in blue rags with a crow perched on her shoulders. The Holly staff that she carries can kill a mortal with just one touch. The Blue Hag is usually seen on the Highlands during the winter months, it is during this time that she is most powerful.
At midnight on May Eve she turns to stone near a Holly tree, there she will stay for six months, until Halloween, when she comes to life again.

The spirits of unbaptised infants are called Tarans in the north east of Scotland.

Scotland

Kelpie: This is another Scottish water faerie which is most often seen as a young black horse loitering near lonely rivers and streams.
It inhabits rivers throughout Scotland, and one is recorded as being banished by St Columba from the River Ness.
Another Kelpie abode is the River Conon (Conan) in Perthshire.
The Kelpie will try and entice you to mount onto its back, and once you are onboard it will dash into the water giving you a dunking in the cold stream.

There is one way a Kelpie can be tamed, its power is said to reside in its bridle. Anybody who could claim the bridle could force the Kelpie to their will.
The Kelpie were greatly prized as they had the strength of 10 horses and the endurance of many more.

Rumour has it that the Mac Gregor clan had in their possession a Kelpie Bridle which had been handed down through the generations from one of their clan who had managed to save himself from a Kelpie near Loch Slochd.

Orkney and Shetland.

The Grey Neighbours: Small grey clad goblins.

Henkies: One of the names given to the Trows

Rannoch Moor, Tayside: Faeries, Ghost Dogs and Water Horses roam the Moors and live beneath the dark silent waters. While walking along the side of the Loch a man found a horse's bridle. It was so beautifully crafted that it must have belonged to a Kelpie.

SCOTLAND

There is another Water Faerie called Each Uisge X very much like the Kelpie which inhabits the Seas and Lochs, although it is much more dangerous as it will devour its victim completely once it has them in the water, except for the liver; which floats to the shore. A sure sign that the Each Uisge had claimed another victim.
Another disguise it takes is that of a handsome man so the locals would be very wary of any lone strangers standing by the side of a Loch.
It can be lured from the water and killed by the smell of roasted meat.

Bean Nighe: The Washing Woman (type of banshee) said to be the spirit of women who die in childbirth.
In appearance she is small in stature always dressed in green and has webbed feet.
She haunts lonely streams in Scotland and Ireland washing the blood stained clothes of people who are about to die.
When her wail is low and sweet a gentle death is in store, when the sound is coarse and loud the death will be violent.
Although often seen as an evil omen it is not always the case; if approached in the right way she can grant wishes. All you have to do is to place yourself between the Bean Nighe and the water. You can ask for three wishes; but in exchange (as is the faerie way) she will ask you three questions, and you will have to answer them truthfully.

Brownies: They covers a large area from the Midlands all the way up to Scotland and the Far Islands. They are small people about three feet high, scruffily dressed in brown clothes with brown faces and shaggy hair.
They are abroad at night finishing the work that has been left undone by the home owner or farmer.
Brownies can become very attached to certain members of their adopted families.
A Brownie who becomes upset at his adopted family, if they have forgotten his bowl of milk or perhaps by having spoken unkindly about his work will sometimes turn into a Boggart.
Boggart can be unkind and like nothing better than causing trouble about the house, poking children and making them cry and being thoroughly unpleasant.
So if you are lucky enough to have a resident Brownie remember its bowl of milk !

A Blacksmith from Raasay lost his teenage daughter to the Each Uisge. It was on the Eve of her wedding day when she was dragged into the loch and devoured. Her Father and intended Husband both vowed revenge on the creature, so they built a forge near the side of the Loch and made a large set of hooks. They then roasted a sheep and heated the hooks until red hot, baited the hooks with the sheep and placed it at the water's edge.
At last a great mist rolled over the water and the Each Uisge rose from the depths and seized the sheep.
The Blacksmith and sweetheart rammed the red hot hooks into the creatures flesh. As it writhed in agony, they drew their swords and killed it.
In the morning there was nothing left of the beast except for a jelly like substance lying in a pool by the side of the Loch.

In parts of Scotland a Curlew is thought to be a long beaked goblin which carries off evil people at night.

SCOTLAND

Sidhe, Sith, or Si (shee): The Gaelic name for Faerie both in the Highlands and Ireland. Tall beings who either appear as shining or opalescent. The former belong to the earthly plane, the latter to the heavenly plane.

The Loch Ness Monster: The most famous of the water Kelpies. This strange legend goes way back into the past, and there are still reports of sightings of Nessie. It has been known as the Great Water Horse, Great Worm and Kelpie.
There are many water monster stories in Scotland and the Kelpie of folklore turns up in many different shapes and sizes but the Great Water Kelpie of Loch Ness is said to be very large and black.

Cu Sith: X Faerie dog found in the Highlands.
The dog is green with long shaggy fur and is the size of a large calf. This dog is not man's best friend and could be dangerous if stumbled upon. It hunts in silence and only barks three times when it has its prey in sight.
The dog is used as a watchdog inside Faerie mounds to keep away intruders.

Cait Sith: X A faerie cat found in the Highlands.
It is as big as a dog and the fur is all black except for a white spot on its breast. Like the dog it can also be ferocious if caught unawares.

There is another water monster legend around Loch Garten, which is in the Abernathy Forest in the Highlands. According to the locals the Loch was haunted by a large flesh eating monster that was a cross between a horse and a bull. It was said to have a jet black mane, huge head and burning eyes.
Its awful roar as it crept out from the Loch at night to hunt could be heard for miles. Local legend tells of a crofter who tried to capture the beast. He tied one end of a long rope to a large boulder that jutted out from the side of the Loch; to the other end a huge hook that he baited with a lamb.
He threw the hook and bait far out into the Loch, then left for home to wait until morning to see what he had caught. That night there was a violent storm, and even though the wind howled and the rain lashed against the side of his croft the man could still hear the monster roaring and screaming in fury. With trembling limbs he returned to the Loch the next morning. All was calm, nothing stirred on the water and nothing could be seen of the monster. The only evidence of the monster being there the night before was a deep groove leading to the waters edge where the huge boulder had been dragged down into the Loch. It is presumed the rock must have dragged it down to the bottom and drowned it, as it was never seen again.

Scotland

The Glaistig: She is a water faerie who is part alluring woman and part goat. She hides her cloven hooves under long flowing gowns. The Faerie uses her good looks to entice men to dance with her and when they are completely under her spell she feeds upon their blood.

But on a gentler note she is kind to children and old people (It's obviously just men that she has a problem with!).

On the Island of Iona women used to leave offerings of milk on the Glaistig Stone every evening, she lived nearby in a hollow rock.

There is another Glaistig Stone Glen in Durer, Appin, where the offerings of milk were also left and in return for this kindness from the local women, this Glaistig would guard their livestock during the night.

Lochaber: A smith once caught a Glaistig and refused to release her until she gave him a herd of cattle; the cattle duly appeared. But the Smith was still not satisfied, he demanded a house that neither enemy or Faerie could harm.

The Glaistig summoned all the Goblins from the surrounding countryside and they set to work building the house for the Smith. It was completed in one night, the last piece was put into place just as the cock crowed. The Goblins disappeared but not the Glaistig as she was still a captive of the Smith.

The Glaistig offered her hand to complete the bargain but the Smith obviously not trusting the Faerie, burnt it with a red hot poker.

The poor Glaistig ran screaming into the hills where she bled to death.

The surrounding plants and ground have ever since been stained red with her blood.

Dunstaffnage Castle. Once the home of a Glaistig, she attached herself to the Campbell Family who owned the Castle.

SCOTLAND

There are many hills that are inhabited by Faeries, here are details of just a few of them.

At Ednam in the Borders is a hill called Pipers Grave, half a mile from the village. Many years ago a Piper from the local band crept inside so that he could learn the Faerie's tunes. He never came out again, but music can be heard sometimes coming from inside the hill. So perhaps he's still practising with the Faeries.

Tomnahurich, Inverness, Highlands.
This wooded hill is where the Faerie Queen Nichiven holds court. Thomas the Rhymer is said to be buried here.

Many would-be Musicians sleep on a Faerie mound in the hope of being transported to Faerieland to be endowed with the gift of Faerie music.

Two mortal fiddlers were hired by the Faerie Queen to play for her guests for one night.
When they were released and stumbled back onto the hillside after playing for the evening, they crumbled to dust, for they had been inside the hillock for 200 years.

SCOTLAND

The hill of Ile in the West Highlands is a Faerie dwelling and here is one of the places the Faerie Queen lives. Here she hands out from a golden goblet, wisdom to all the women of the world.
"Still on the hill when the wisdom was handed out" is the local saying for anybody less than bright.

Scotland

True Thomas The Rhymer: Many people have been seduced into leaving the mortal world and travelling to Faerieland; some never to be seen again, for once there it is very difficult to escape. One such was Thomas the young Laird of Erceldoune who one May Day saw a beautiful woman riding towards him across the grass. He was so smitten by the woman that he promised then and there to love and stay with her for ever if she would only give him a kiss: although in some versions it's more than a kiss he received! Once the kiss had been given Thomas watched in horror as the woman's appearance changed before his eyes, her hair turned gray and her face became lined and haggard, her clothes became tattered and there before him stood an old crone where two minutes before there had been the beautiful woman with whom he had fallen in love.

Thomas knew that he could not go back on his promise and as she made to leave the hill where they had met, he gave one backward glance to the mortal world. Then followed the old crone to a cave in the side of Eildon Hill and from there into the otherworld. They travelled for many days in pitch black surrounded by strange sounds until at last they came to an enormous cavern and in the middle stood a Faerie Castle surrounded by a beautiful garden. Thomas turned to the old crone to exclaim at the wonder of the place and there in place of the old crone stood the beautiful woman as she had been before. Thomas gazing on her face then knew that it was the Faerie Queen herself that he had made his promise to. To Thomas, it seemed as though he had only been there for a few days and when the Faerie Queen told him that in fact he had been there for seven years he could not believe it. She warned him that if he stayed another night then he would be bound for ever in Faerieland and for the sake of their love he would be given a chance to return to his mortal home. With a blink of her eye Thomas found himself once again standing on Huntlie Bank. The Faerie Queen gave Thomas a parting gift: the ability to be a master harpist and also that he would answer every question with truth. For seven years his wisdom and prophecies were sought by many. But he never forgot the beautiful Queen that had stolen his heart; and one day he received a summons from her; Thomas walked out of his home and was never seen again in the mortal world.

True Thomas was said to have foretold the crowning of Robert the Bruce and the Battle of Flodden in 1513.

He also prophesied that James VI of Scotland would gain the English throne after Elizabeth I death in 1603.

"When Tweed and Powsail meet at Merlins Grave then England and Scotland shall one monarch have"

These two rivers flooded after the old Queens death and came together at the ancient stone.

SCOTLAND

SCOTLAND

The Ballad of True Thomas

True Thomas lay on the grassy bank,
   And he beheld a lady gay.
   A lady that was brisk and bold,
To come riding o'er the ferny brae.

Her skirt was of the grass green silk,
   Her mantle of the velvet fine,
And on every lock of her horse's mane,
   Hung fifty silver bell and nine.

True Thomas he took off his hat,
   And bowed low down to his knee,
All hail thou virgin, Queen of Heaven,
   For your like on Earth I ne'er did see.

Oh no, oh no, True Thomas she said,
   That name does not belong to me,
I am but the Queen of Fair Elfland
That has come for to visit here with thee.

And you must go with me now, Thomas,
   True Thomas you must go with me,
And you must serve me seven years,
Through good or ill as may chance to be.

She turned about her milk white steed
   And took True Thomas up behind,
   And aye when'er the bridle rang,
   The steed flew faster than the wind,

For forty days and forty nights,
They wade through red blood to the knee,
   And he saw neither sun nor moon,
   But heard the roaring of the sea.

Oh they rode on and further on,
   Until they came to a garden tree,
Light down, light down, you lady fair,
   And I'll pull off that fruit for thee.

Oh no, oh no, True Thomas she says,
   That fruit may not be touched by thee,
   For all the plagues that are in hell
Are upon the fruit of this country.

But I have bread here in my lap,
   Likewise a bottle of red wine,
And before that we go further on,
We shall rest, and you may dine.

When he had eaten and drunk his fill,
She said Lay your head down on my knee.
And before we climb yon high high hill,
   I will show you wonders three.

Oh do you see that broad broad road
   That lies by the lily leven?
   Oh that is the road of wickedness,
Though some call it the road to Heaven.

And do you see that narrow narrow road
   All beset with thorns and briars?
   Oh that is the way of righteousness,
   Though after it few enquire.

And do you see that bonny bonny road
   Which winds about the ferny brae?
   Oh that is the road to Fair Elfland,
And together there you and I will go.

But Thomas you must hold your tongue
   Whatever you may hear or see...
For if one word you chance to speak,
You will never get back to your own country.

And he has gotten a coat of woven cloth,
   Likewise the shoes of velvet green,
And till seven years were past and gone,
   True Thomas ne'er on earth was seen.

SCOTLAND

Sluagh: X These are the most most formidable of the Scottish Faeries, considered by some to be fallen angels. They fly nightly over the earth spreading sickness and injury to the mortals below, they also fight amongst themselves during the winter months and where ever their blood falls down to earth a bright red Lichen called Crotal will grow.

SCOTLAND

Avoch, Highlands. Craigie Well, Munlochy Bay.
Its waters can be used as protection against evil magic and spirits, but to do so, it must be visited on the first Sunday in May.

Durness, Highlands.
On the coast is Smoo Cave, a three chambered cave which is another entrance to the Otherworld.

Tonnahurich, Highlands:
This hill is now covered by a cemetery but it used to be a very busy Faerie site. They used to meet here for their revels in the Autumn. It is also the spot where Thomas the Rhymer returned from his visit to Elfhame; Faerieland.

Doon Hill, Aberfoyle:
This area is strongly associated with the Rev Robert Kirk the author of The Secret Commonwealth, written in 1691.
This book was written about the Faerie world and he was said to have been taken away as punishment for daring to write about them.
The Reverend's spirit was imprisoned in a Pine on the local Faerie hill.
This is easily found by following the path from the Church up Doon Hill to the clearing where the Pine stands.
(The path is marked from Gartmere as 'the Faerie Trail')

On the Isle of Lewis Fishermen pour a barrel of Ale onto the waves at Halloween so that the Sea Spirits will grant them a good catch through the year.

Kit with the Candlestick is the Scottish Will o the Wisp.

Nuggie: Water Kelpie from the Shetlands.

In the 16th C, Girdle Measuring was a common practice for wise women to see if evil spirits or Faeries had invaded a person's body.
Any unexplained weight gain especially after an illness was considered very suspicious. The affected person's girdle or belt would be measured then charms and incantations would be said over it. It would be then measured again, if the belt did not show a reduction in size it would be chopped into bits and buried. This was supposed to be a sure fire way of getting rid of unwanted Possesions.
(I wonder if the 'wise women' made new belts as well?)

Faeries come in all shapes and sizes.

SCOTLAND

The Grugach is a kindhearted guardian of grazing animals, leading them to water and protecting them from harm.
Although she is rather ugly she is always welcomed into crofters home so that she can seek warmth at their fires, as she also brings good luck with her.

Up until the 1900s in the Scottish Islands milk would be poured into hollow stones as offerings to her.

SCOTLAND

Dun Bhuirg, Kilfinichon, Strathclyde:
Many years ago a woman weaver lived near this Faerie Fort, she once complained loudly near the mound that it was high time that the people in the hill helped her with her weaving.
She returned home to find the Croft full of the little people from the mound busy weaving.
They produced a vast quantity of excellent cloth for her but to the discomfort of the woman then demanded payment for their labours.
The crafty old woman tricked them by shouting that Dun Bhuirg was on fire.
The little Faeries rushed back in panic to the Faerie fort to find they had been tricked.
But they had the last laugh; once the old lady went to take the cloth to market all she found was a pile of ashes instead of the cloth.

Balbeggie, Abernyte, Tayside:
The Sidlaws of Shian Hill, a very powerful Faerie hill, this is one of the major strongholds for all Faerie beings in the district.

Shelley: He is a Bogie that lives in streams.
He is fond of wearing strings of shells draped around him, so you can clearly hear him coming, which is a real bonus as he enjoys tricking travellers and misleading them.

The Altmor Burn near Claich foldich in Perthshire is haunted by a Brownie called Puddlefoot.
He stays hidden in the water until night when everything is quiet in the nearby farm, he then creeps his way up to the house to clean and tidy.

Some consider it unlucky to talk about Faeries so use nicknames for the 'little people'.
Anybody spying on them are often blinded.

Stones have many magical and healing powers.
Stones with holes in them are especially lucky, and if you are lucky enough to find one in running water it is doubly lucky and should be buried beneath your doorstep.

SCOTLAND

The Standing Stones of Callanish, on the Isle of Lewis, Outer Hebrides:
This is one of the most impressive and the most remote stone circles, it is situated on the hill overlooking Loch Roag on the west coast of the Island.
It was erected 5,000 years ago for religious and magical ceremonies.
In the centre is a giant monolith, 5 metres high, underneath is which a small chambered cairn.
Surrounding this is a circle of thirteen stones, from this central point avenues of stones radiate North, South, East and West.
From the air it resembles a giant Celtic cross, 120 metres long and 46 metres wide.
Up until the 19th Century local people still visited the stones to celebrate Beltane and Midsummer (even though the local minister forbade these gatherings) it was believed that it would not do to 'neglect the stones'.
At the dawn of the midsummer Solstice a glowing figure walks through the northern avenue, this sight is preceded by the call of a Cuckoo.

Many people believe that this stone circle was used to calculate the movement of the moon from one solstice to another by aligning individual stones with points on the horizon.

There are many legends associated with these stones, one is that they are giants turned to stone by St Kieran for refusing to be converted to Christianity.

SCOTLAND

Duergar: Northern Dwarves that dress in lamb and moleskins. They guard the old Faerie paths and can be rather malevolent to travellers, often removing or turning signposts to ensure the hapless person will get lost.

It seems to be one of the Faerie ways that if a human being offers to exchange a possession of his for anything that belongs to the Faeries then they cannot refuse however bad a deal it may be for them.
John Roy of Glenbrarn in Badanoch used this knowledge to his advantage when he saw a group of Faeries fly over him carrying something. He threw his hat into the air and called out "Mine be yours and yours be mine".
Although the Faeries were furious, they had to take the bargain and dropped their prize at his feet.
Their prize turned out to be a woman, that had been taken from her home many miles away, for she spoke no language that John Roy could understand.
After many years of living with John and his family and learning the language it turned out that she was English. She was successfully reunited with her family after a chance meeting with her son.
The woman's family had thought that she had died as the Faeries had left a changeling in her place. This had later sickened and died.

Dryads: (The name comes from the Greek druas meaning Oak, the ruling tree of the woods)
These are female tree spirits, they have strong affinities with the Willow, Oak and Ash. The Dryads will emerge at night and roam around the woods, their beautiful singing can be heard throughout the wood.
Hamadryads remain within the same tree, usually Oaks, for as long as the tree lives, and if their tree is cut down they will die.
Dryads and Hamadryads are sometimes seen as beautiful women from the waist up but the rest of their body resembles trunks and roots.

Wag at the Wall: A Scottish Border spirit, a domestic friendly Faerie that attaches itself to a particular family although it is much feared in the Borders.
It is considered unlucky to swing an empty pot hook hanging from the chimney as it would be an invitation for the Wag at the Wall to sit there.

Isobel Gowdie A 17th Century Witch claimed to have to have received all of her knowledge of witchcraft from the Faeries. She also said that she used elfshot to wound and kill neighbours that had annoyed her.

Elves

Elves: In Scotland the Faeries of human size are called Elves, they live in troops, have Kings and Queens and are skilled in the use of magic. Their Faerieland is called Elfhame.

In England it is the smaller Trooping Fay who are called Elves and the name is applied particularly to the small Faerie boys.
The Elves emerge at night and sing and dance in the light of the full moon, their beautiful music is said to bring the trees and rocks to life so that they too will dance under the moon.
Any mortal that hears the tune The Elf Kings Reel will also fall under the spell and dance until the morning, the only way to break the enchantment is to cut the strings of the fiddle.

In North Yorkshire if the cattle become restless or agitated it is believed that Elves are shooting at them. If an animal begins to sicken the only way to cure an Elf shot beast is to collect the arrow heads and to dip them into water, stir it nine times and then make the animal drink the water.
(One test to see if the animal has been elf shot is to pass a large needle through different parts of its body. If it does not bleed it is a sign that it is bleeding internally from the elf shot)

The Tree Elves of Scotland are small delicate creatures that dress entirely in green. They are experts in the use of herbs and use their skills to help the wildlife of the woods and hills.

The small round fossils known as Achinite has been thought for many years to be Faerie Loaves, and the Flint arrow heads found around many prehistoric sites to be Faerie darts or Elf shots.

If you find an elf shot look after it well for it will protect you from harm, never throw it away for they will come to retrieve the shot and take you along with it.

Elf winds blowing on a mortal will sometimes cause an irritating rash, this can only be cured by rubbing the affected area with a Bible.

SCOTLAND

Claypots Castle at Broughty Ferry, Tayside used to be the home of a Brownie. He did all the chores about the place in return for a bowl of cream.
But there was one thing the hard working Brownie couldn't stand and that was lazy servants.
The Brownie became so cross with one particular kitchen maid that he beat her with some cabbage stalks. Then stormed out of the castle cursing the house and occupants never to be seen again.
(I have heard that he has moved in with a nice family around the Glasgow area!)

The Aberdeen Brownies have no separate toes or fingers.
In the Scottish lowlands they have a hole instead of a nose, while some have no mouths just huge noses.

Bodesbeck Farm, Dumfries and Gall:
This farm situated near Moffat was very prosperous due to a hard working Brownie that lived there.
After an exceptionally good harvest one year the Farmer wished to give the Brownie a reward for all his hard work.
So he left a loaf of bread and a pan of cream out for the Brownie instead of the usual bread and water.
But the Farmer found to his cost that Brownies are easily offended for he stormed off the Farm shouting over his shoulder as he went,

Ca' Brownie Ca
A' the luck of Bodesbeck
Awa' tae Leithen Ha.

SCOTLAND

Faerie's Cradle, Hetton-le-Hole. Tyne and Wear: Faeries dance around this barrow on Moonlit nights.

Faerie Folk Hillock, Carmyle, Srathclyde: Faerie revels are held on top of this Tumulous.

Blue men of the Minch: these are blue sea creatures that live around the Scottish Isles, they delight in keeping the waters of the Minch in turmoil, causing storms and shipwrecks unless the unlucky sailors can best them in a guessing game.

A hundred years ago a Brownie called Hairy Meg lived in the farmhouse of Achnarrow near Glenlivet.
As per usual the Brownie did all the work and was regularly rewarded with a bowl of milk and a piece of oat cake.
After a particularly bad year on the farm, the crops failed and the animals died, the farmer decided he couldn't afford to keep the rest of the servants. So he sacked them, much to Hairy Meg's disgust. She was so upset that she went on strike, refusing to do any of the chores and throwing pots and pans around the farm house.
Hairy Meg made such a nuisance of herself that the Farmer had to relent and give all the servants back their jobs, and immediately Hairy Meg regained her temper.

SCOTLAND

Trows: They are often confused with the Orkney Hogboon or Hogboy, although they are not so nasty. Trows appear similar to humans although the Peerie Trows are small enough to shelter under leaves. The larger Trows have a nasty habit of carrying off young girls and midwives.

The Trows of Shetland are very keen dancers, their lack of grace is made up for by their great enthusiasm.
There is a story of a Trow woman who gatecrashed a couple's wedding celebrations, unable to watch the festivities any longer without joining in she burst into the hall, and began dancing in the usual henking fashion of the Trows.
Squatting down holding her hands tightly between her thighs and calves she hopped up and down the hall impatiently waiting for one of the mortal men to join her.
When no one volunteered she became rather peeved and began whirling around and around chanting,
"Hey! Co Cuttie; and ho co Cuttie
An Wha" thee dance wi me co Cuttie
I luke aboot an sae naeboody
Sae I'll henk on mesain, co Cuttie"

until breathless she gave
up on the mortal men
as a bad job and vanished.

On Yule Eve when Trows are very active, it is the custom to unlock every lock in the house as Trows hate locked doors and will break them open. They are frequent visitors to crofts and they terrify the inhabitants enough without the added bonus of smashing the doors down.

Trows have the ability to make themselves invisible, to break this spell you have to hold your sweetheart's hand or stand on their feet.

Haltadans, Fetlar, Shetland:
Here the Trows used to hold their reels and feasts. During one such feast they were having such a good time that they forgot the time and carried on dancing.
The sun rose and they were all turned to stone.
The name of the double circle of stones that stand there now means
The Limping Dance..

Some of the most well known Scottish dance tunes were inspired from listening outside Faerie hills. In Shetland the most famous is the Trowie Reel, this was heard by an old fiddler while he rested on the Faerie Hill of Gulla Hammar.

SCOTLAND

The Hogboy of Orkney inhabits Burial Mounds, and they are often left gifts of food and drink.
It is best not to disturb their mounds as they will take their revenge by killing the local livestock.

Silent Moving Folk: The Scottish fairies who live in green knolls and in the depths of the mountains.

The Frid in the Highlands are responsible for the fertility of the land so offerings of milk are regularly given to them.
It is wise not to speak of them as they can hear whatever is said when the wind blows.

The Ghillie Dhu are tree spirits that live mainly in Birch thickets, hiding amongst the moss and leaves to avoid the sight of mortals.
They are best avoided as they can be very unfriendly and have been known to capture people, tie them up with ropes of ivy and then take them off to Faerieland.

There is an old well on the slopes of Schiehallion "The Faerie Hill of the Caledonians" at the eastern end of Rannoch Moor.
It is inhabited by Fairies who grant wishes and can cure all sicknesses.
It used to be visited every May Day by the local girls who would offer flowers to the Fairies to bring them good luck.

Fairies live in the burn of Invernauld and the nearby hill. A man once heard music coming from a cave in the hillside.
He entered and was not found until a year later, still dancing to the music of the Faerie piper.

Lorntie/ Lornty Perthshire: The Laird of Lorntie had a dangerous encounter with a freshwater Mermaid who was crying for help in Loch Benachally near his castle. He plunged into the water to save her but was pulled back by his servant who recognised her as a Mermaid.
She was furious and cursing raised herself out of the water screaming at him, "Lorntie, Lorntie
Were it not for your man, I'd have your heart's blood in my pan."
This Mermaid was obviously a blood drinker.
(See also Page 76)

Scotland

Urisk is another solitary faerie that lives north of the border, haunting lonely pools. He likes human company but he has such a peculiar appearance that most chance travellers take to their heels when they spot him. The Urisks meet up at particular times of the year, a corrie near Loch Katrine is one spot for their very solemn gatherings.

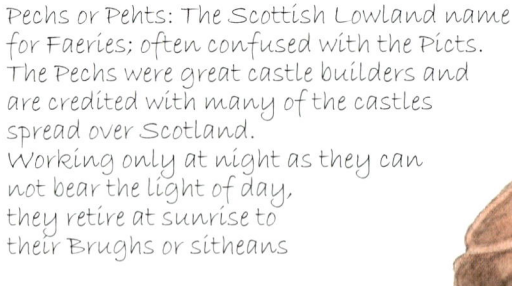

Pechs or Pehts: The Scottish Lowland name for Faeries; often confused with the Picts. The Pechs were great castle builders and are credited with many of the castles spread over Scotland.
Working only at night as they can not bear the light of day, they retire at sunrise to their Brughs or sitheans

Redcap: X Well known for being the most evil of the Border Goblins. He is short and wiry with ragged pointy teeth and sharp claws like steel.
He lives in old abandoned castles and towers, especially those with a violent history.
Hermitage Castle in Roxburgh shire where Lord Soulis (a man with an evil reputation) lived was said to have had a red cap as a familiar.
Redcap murders by rolling boulders down onto their victims or tearing at them with his sharp claws and then he drinks their blood.
Dyes his cap in human blood hence his name!.

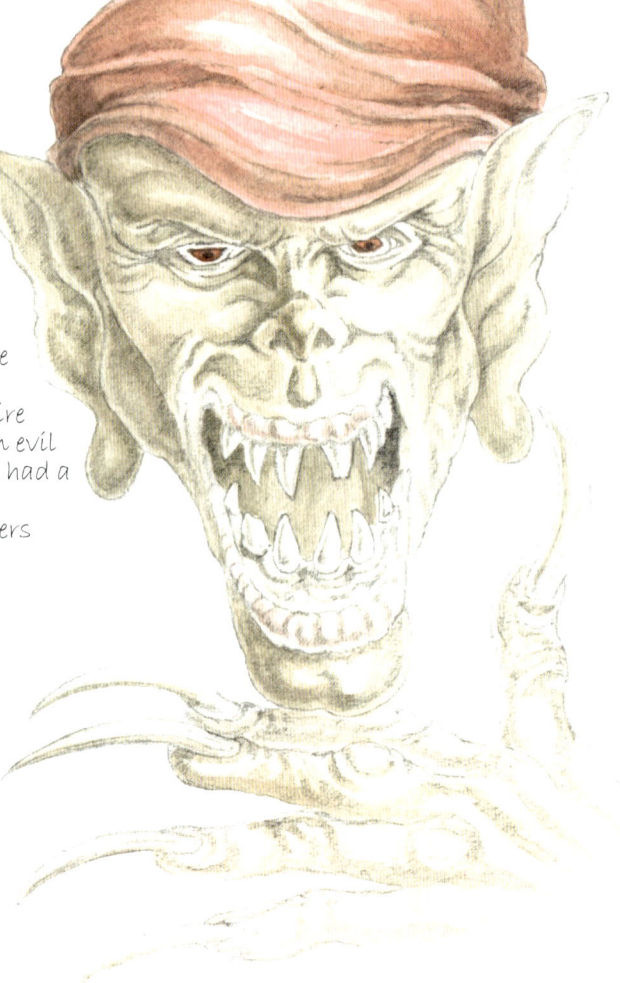

The Breadalbane Hills are home to the Urisks who summer in the hills but travel down to the valleys in the winter. They work on the more secluded farms in return for milk and clothes.
The waterfall near Clifton is called the Cascade of the Urisk.

SCOTLAND

Dunvegan Castle, Skye:
The MacCleods of Dunvegan can trace their ancestry back to the 14th Century when a Faerie wife of a Chief gave her husband a Faerie flag as a gift before she returned to Faerieland
The belief is that if the Clan is in peril they can become invincible by unfurling the Faerie flag. but it can only be used three times and they have already used it twice.
The first in 1490 in a battle against the MacDonalds, and the second in 1520 in yet another battle against the Clanradd branch of the MacDonalds.
During the Second World War many clansmen carried a photo of the flag off to war with them as a lucky charm.
The flag is now kept in the Drawing Room of Dunvegan Castle.

Dun Borve, Snizort, Skye:
The villagers here wanted to get rid of the Faeries who lived in the old fort, so they called out that the fort was burning, when the Faeries rushed out of the fort to escape the flames they realised they had been tricked and left the Island in rage. It has to be said that the villagers grew to regret their actions as the village never prospered after the Faeries departure.

Dun Osdale, Duirinish, Skye:
A member of the MacCleod Clan was invited to a Faerie Banquet at this fort. While he was there he was offered a drink from a golden cup, but he knew better than to drink it so he tipped the wine away into the grass and then ran off with the golden cup!

The Fachan of Glen Etire, Strathclyde is a peculiar sight with one hand out of his chest, one leg out of his bottom and one eye in the middle of his head.

Spitting is a great defence against bad luck and evil spirits.
So you can either spit in your right shoe every morning, spit on your chest or spit three times on the ground while passing dangerous places.
Spittle is also very powerful in protecting children from Faerie abduction.

Branches of Ash, Rowan, Birch Hazel, Holly, Oak, Hawthorne and Bay are placed around doors of buildings to repel Faeries.

Well spirits are shape shifters, they often take the form of beautiful girls dressed in white.
The wells are a source of healing especially for women, dealing with fertility problems and young girls would visit the wells hoping to dream of their future husbands.

Scotland

One legendary Faerie gift was given to a MacCrimmon, Pipers to the MacCleods of Dunvegan in Skye.
Many years ago a young man from the MacCrimmon family stumbled into a Faerie hill, he was naturally concerned when he found himself surrounded by hostile Faeries but the mischievous creatures decided they would do him no harm, just play a little game. So they offered him a choice: prosperity without skill, or skill without prosperity.
The young man chose the gift of skill and the Faeries handed him a gift of a set of Bagpipes.
When he played these pipes it produced the most amazing music and for hundreds of years after the family of MacCrimmon were renowned on Skye for their playing and composing.

The MacEachern family of Islay were skilled Smiths and armourers and the reputation for their work spread far and wide but it was nothing compared to the work they produced following the kidnapping of one of their sons by a troupe of Faeries. The Father followed the Faeries back to their enchanted hill and found his son working at a forge deep in the Faerie hill. Although the man begged for them to release his son they refused and hustled him outside the hill, just as they released their hold on the Father's arm a cock crowed and their magical hold on the boy was broken. The young Mac Eachern rushed out into the early morning light to where his Father was standing on the side of the Faerie mound, he was unhurt by his encounter with the little people although he never mentioned his adventure deep in the Faerie tunnels. But one day, some time after this occurred he was watching his Father at the family forge, without a word he took the tools from his Father and started making a beautiful guard, which was to fit the hilt of the sword of Islay. The designs on this were like nothing the Family had ever seen before. The boy continued producing beautiful Faerie inspired work for many years and became renowned throughout Scotland.

Horseshoes have a twofold use.
Traditionally nailed over doorways of houses, stables and churches, If nailed with the ends pointing downwards it will prevent evil spirits from crossing the threshold. For good luck the horseshoe must be nailed with the ends upwards to prevent the luck from spilling out.

If nailed to a bed it will prevent nightmares.

The horseshoes must never be removed once they are in place.

Cocks are a symbol of light and goodness, they have the power to banish evil and they also bring good luck and fertility.

Come out from your Faerie bower
Come upon this golden hour
Come to us we beg you please
Faeries dance among the breeze

Other Faerie Sites

Fairy's Toot, Butcombe, Avon.
Although this chamber tomb has been destroyed for many years it is still home to Faeries, Goblins and Ghosts.

Inkberrow, Hereford and Worcester.
The Faeries left here after the church bells were installed, as Faeries cannot stand the sound of them.
A Faerie called out as they departed,
"Neither sleep, neither lie,
Inkberrows ting tang hangs so high".

Fairy Stone, Warden, Northumberland.
The cavity in this stone is known as the Fairy Trough.
The stone is one of four that mark the boundary of the village.

Fairy Hill, Brinkburn, Northumberland.
This hill is supposed to be one of the last burial places of the Faeries.

Frensham, Surrey.
In the 13th century Church here there is a huge Cauldron which is one yard in diameter. It was borrowed from the Faeries and never returned and because of this the Faeries of Frensham have never lent any thing again.

A Mermaid inhabits the Aqualate Mere in Staffordshire but she is only seen when a calamity is about to happen. She moved to this mere after her original home in Newport dried up. Workmen that were busy dredging the mere one day were astonished when the Mermaid rose from the water and warned them that if this mere dried up as well she would destroy the local town of Newport.

Boggart Hole Clough at Blackley Greater Manchester is inhabited by a Boggart.
Although Boggart Hall his original home has been demolished he still remains haunting the area.

The Black Dog of Birdlip Hill Gloucestershire is rather different from the usual phantom dogs which bring death to anybody that sees them, this Black Dog will aid lost travellers and guide them on their way.

When the new church bell was being transported to Marden in Herefordshire to be hung, it slipped from its ropes and fell into the river. The workmen tried to haul the bell from the water but it was held fast by the Mermaid that lived in the river.
The Church wardens consulted the local wise man who told them how to retrieve the bell but he warned that it had to be done in silence.
The workmen silently gathered at the river bank and began hauling the bell towards the surface with the Mermaid still fast asleep inside the bell. It was just nearing the river bank when one other workmen shouted out:
"In spite of all the devils in hell now we'll land Marden's great bell!". This woke the Mermaid who bit through the thick ropes holding the bell and pulled it back down into the water.
If the weather is clear and calm on a Sunday morning the bell can be heard ringing in response to the other church bells.

A cave at Rosebury Rock near Lulsley in Worcestershire was inhabited by the Faeries.

OTHER FAERIE SITES

A cave at Rosebury Rock near Lulsley in Worcestershire was inhabited by the Faeries. It was common for women to leave broken baking peels from the home by the entrance of the cave and when they returned in the morning it would have been mended.

Meon Hill in Warwickshire is haunted by a Black Dog. It was last seen in 1945 by a Scotland Yard Superintendent who had been called in to help with the strange murder of a farm labourer called Charles Walton. The man was known to be involved in witchcraft and the locals believed that his strange death which occurred on the 2nd February, Candlemas, was part of a witchcraft Festival.
He had been found pinned by his neck to the ground with his pitchfork, and his billhook had been used to slash a cross into his chest.
Walton was known to have seen the Black Dog many times roaming around Meon Hill.

The River Trent is the home of a little Boggart who paddles himself about on the water in a little round boat. He is usually found at bend of the river between Wildsworth and Owston Ferrry on the Humberside /Lincolnshire border.
The Boggart make the other mortal boatmen very wary of using the river at night and most preferred to moor their boats elsewhere.

Offerings of cheese used to be thrown into the waters of the Cheese Well, Minchmoor, Peebles as offerings for the Faeries, as they controlled the well's powers and could grant wishes and sometimes cure illness.

check list

Cornwall Page 9
Muryan..
Cornish Knockers............................
Portunes...
Devils Dandy Dogs...........................
Mermaid of Lamorna........................
Mermaid of Zennor..........................
Mermaid of Padstow........................
The Whooper...................................
Morgawr..
Spriggan...
Terry Tom Tit Tot.............................
Faeries of Selena Moor....................
Will o the Wisp.................................
Pixies..
Devon Page 22
Yeth Hounds....................................
Black Dog of Uplyme.......................
Pixies of Dartmoor...........................
Somerset Page 25
Oak Men...
Chimbley Charlie..............................
Hunkey Punk....................................
Spunky of Taunton...........................
Griggs...
The Woman of the Mist...................
The White Lady of Wellow...............
Apple Tree Man................................
Colt Pixy...
Lazy Lawrence.................................
Spunkies..
Gwynn ap Nudd...............................
Wild Hunt...
Pixies of Stogursey..........................
Dorset Page 36
Black Dog Portland..........................
Spectral Army..................................
Water Spirits of Frome....................
Faerie Horde of Eggardon...............
Faeries of the Music Barrows.........
Veasta..
Gabbygammies................................
Stourpaine Faeries..........................
Colpexies...
Nanny Diamonds..............................
Lazy Lawrence.................................

Guernsey Page 42
Faeries of St Peter...........................
Tchi-Co...
Jersey Page 42
Black Dog St Peter Port...................
Dog of Bouley...................................
Faerie Bridal party at Hanois...........
Sussex Page 44
Snake of Cissbury Ring...................
Spirits of Chanctonbury Ring..........
Wiltshire Page 49
Faeries of Avebury...........................
Faeries and spirits of West Kennett......
Faeries of Hackpen Hill...................
Oxfordshire Page 51
Faeries of Rollright..........................
Witch of Rollright.............................
Buckinghamshire Page 53
Goblins of Shucklow Warren...........
Suffolk Page 54
Malekin...
Faeries of Stowmarket....................
Cambridgeshire Page 60
Jack o Lantern.................................
Shug Monkey...................................
Yallery Brown...................................
Tiddy Ones......................................
Black Shuck.....................................
Hyster sprites..................................
Gnomes..
Wales Page 64
Water Leaper...................................
Coblynau..
Ellyllon..
Gwyllion..
Verry Volk..
The Green Lady Of Caerphilly.........
Plant Rhys Pwfen............................
Tywyth Teg......................................
Bendith y Maman............................
Goblins of Bryn y Elyllon..................
Three Sisters of Tangrogo..............
Bwbachod..
Lake Maidens of Myddfai.................
Gwarwyn a Throt.............................
Cwn Annwn......................................

Check List

Ellylldon..
Gwragedd Annwn................................
Mermaid of Llanychaiarn.........................
Sea Faeries of Milford Haven...................
Mermaid of Carreg Ina.............................
Faeries and Goblins of
 Llyn Du'r Arddu....................................
Lady of the Lake of Llyn Fawr.................
Faeries of Llyn Fan Fach..........................
Faeries and village of
Cwm yr Eglwys..
Nymphs...
Shropshire   Page 74
Mermaid of Childs Ercall..........................
Wild Eric..
Magical Cow of Mitchells Fold.................
Lincolnshire   Page 76
Strangers..
LincolnshireBrownies..............................
Derbyshire   Page 77
Goblin of Hobs Hurst House....................
Hob of Topley Pike..................................
Mermaid of Kinder Scout.........................
Peggy wi the Lantern...............................
Cheshire   Page 79
Mermaid of Rostherne Mere......................
Lancashire   Page 80
Faerie procession at
 Higher Penworthen................................
Mermaid of Black Rock............................
Kilmoulis..
Boggart of Longridge................................
Padfoot...
Water Spirit of River Kibble.....................
Yorkshire   Page 83
Hobgoblins...
Jenny Greenteeth.....................................
Peg Powler...
Hob of Runswick Bay...............................
Faeries of Willy Howe..............................
Haliwell Boggle..
Boggart...
Bogles..
Goblins..
Faeries of Elbolton Hill.............................
Faeries of Pudding Pie Hill.......................
Jeanie the Bogle of Mulgrave Wood.........

Cumbria   Page 88
Faeries of Hardnott Pass..........................
The Dead at Beetham..............................
Faerie Castle of Bassenthwaite Lake.
Northumberland   Page 92
Hedley Kow..
The Cauld Lad...
Faeries of Rothley....................................
Ireland   Page 94
Leprechaun..
Merrows...
Banshees of Lough Gur............................
Dead Hunt of Lough Gur.........................
Tuatha de Danann....................................
Faeries of Cnoc Aine................................
Faeries of Cnoc Firinne............................
Daniel O Donoghue..................................
Pookas..
The Gentry...
Fir Darrig...
Lunantishness..
Fear Garta..
Dublachan..
Tash ....
Leanhaun Shee...
Picts...
Daoine Sidhe..
Firbolgs..
Formorians...
Bean Tighe...
Fear Dearc..
Gancener..
Ballybog...
Bean Sidhe...
Bean Fionn...
Horses of the Tuatha de Danann..............
Clurican...
Aine of Lough Gur...................................
Finvarra and Oonagh................................
Isle of Man   Page 104
Cabbyl Ushtey..
Tarroo Ushtey..
Faerie Cattle..
The Manx Fendoree..................................
Shan Cashtel..
The Glashans...
Buggane...

check list

Faeries of Faerie Hill..............................
Phynnodderee...
Howlaa Manx..
Shoopi Hee..
Faeries of Ballana Bridge.......................
Spirit of Nikkesens Pool........................

Scotland   Page 110

Selkies...
Mermaid of Portgordon..........................
The Nuckalavee....................................
Urisks..
Kelpie..
Faeries of Rannoch Moor.......................
Each Usigge..
Bean Nighe..
Brownies...
Sidhe Sith..
The Loch Ness Monster.........................
Cu Sith..
Cait Sith..
The Glaistig..
Faeries of Ile...
Faerie Queen of Tomnahunch................
Sluagh...
Kit with the Candlestick.........................
Nuggie..
The Gruagach...
Faeries of Dun Bhuirg............................
Faeries of Shian Hill...............................
Shelley..
Duergar...
Wag at the Wall......................................
Dryads..
Elves...
Aberdeen Brownies...............................
Hairy Meg...
Faeries of Faerie Folk Hillock................
Blue Men of the Minch...........................

Trows..
The Hogboy of Orkney..........................
Silent Moving Folk.................................
The Frid..
Faeries of Schiehallion Well...................
Faeries of the Burn ....
Gillie Dhu...

Brown Man of the Muirs........................
Pechs..
Redcap..
The Fachan...

ADDITIONAL READING

Readers Digest Folklore Myths and Legends (London 1973)
Mermaids, Beatrice Philpotts (Random House New York 1980)
Ireland, a sacred journey Michael Dames (London 2000)
Celtic Mythology, T.W. Rolleston (Dover Publications 1917)
Sacred Britain, M. Palmer and N. Palmer (Piatkus London 1997)
British Folklore Myths and Legends, Marc Alexander (Sutton Publishing 1982)
Troublesome Things, A history of Fairies and Fairy stories, Diane Purkiss (Allen Lane 2001)
The Encyclopedia of witches and witchcraft, Rosemary Ellen Guiley (USA 1989)
Faeries, Brian Froud. (Pan Books London 1978)
Vanishing People, Katherine Briggs (Pantheon Books 1978)
The Book of Faeries, Frances Melville (Fairwinds Press USA 2002)
Faeries in Nineteenth Century art and literature, Nicola Bown (Cambridge University Press 2001)
Everymans Book of English Folk Tales, Sybil Marshall (J.M Dent &Son Ltd London 1981)
A complete guide to Fairies and magical beings, Cassandra Eason (Judy Paitkus Ltd London 2001)
Celtic Britain, Homer Sykes (Weidenfield & Nicolson Ltd 1997)
Chronicles of the Celts, Ian Zaczek (Collins & Brown Ltd London 1996)
A Dictionary of Monsters and Mysterious Beasts, Carey Miller (Pan Books London 1974)
Gnomes, W.Huygen & R. Poortvliet (Netherlands 1976)
The Little Book of Celtic Myths & Legends, K&J Taylor (Parragon Bath 1999)
The Illustrated Encyclopedia of Arthurian Legends, Ronan Coghlan (Barnes & Noble with Element 1995)
Legends of Devon, Sally Jones (Bossiney Books Bodmin Cornwall 1981)
Legends of Dorset, Polly Lloyd (Bossiney Books Bodmin Cornwall 1988)
Myths & Legends of the British Isles, Richard Barber (Boydell & Brewer Ltd Suffolk 1999)
Mushrooms, Michael Chinnery (Granada Publishing Ltd London 1983)
Tree Wisdom, Jacqueline M Paterson (Thorsons London 1996)
The Enchanted Land, Janet & Colin Bord (Thorsons London 1995)
Seafaring Lore &Legend, Peter D Jeans (USA 2004)
Calendar of Garden Lore, Julia Jones & Barbera Deer (Dorling Kindersley London 1989)
The Pixy Book, Frances Cockerton (Tor Mark Press Penryn 1996)
Tales of Dartmoor Pixies, William Crossing (Newcastle upon Tyne 1890)
Leylines, Philip Heselton (Hodder & Stoughton London 1999)
Treasures of Britain (Drive Publications Ltd London 1968)
Wild Flowers of Britain, Roger Phillips (Pan Books London 1977)

Believe in the Faeries
Who make the dreams come true
Believe in the wonder,
The Stars and the Moon,
Believe in the magic,
From Faerie above,
They dance on the flowers
And sing songs of love.
And if you just believe,
And always stay true,
The Faeries will be there,
To watch over you.

Anon

INDEX

Aine 96
Alder 47
All Hallows Eve 34,100
All Saints Day 21
Amber 82
Angels 7,108
Annwyn 33
Apple 47, 58
Apple Tree Man 30, 58
Arthur 32
Ash 5, 47,132
Avalon 32

Ballybog 99
Banshees 29, 93,100,112
Bay 132
Bean Fionn 100
Bean Nighe 112
Bean Sidhe 100
Bean Tighe 99
Beltane 21
Bwca 10
Belemnites 38
Bendith y Maman 63
Betws Garman 62
Birch 21, 132
Blackberries 47
Black Dog 43,135,136
Black Shuck 58
Bluebells 47
Blue Men of the Minch 128
Blue Burches 28
Blue Hag 29,110
Boggart 78,82,112,135,136
Bogle 72,82,83,90
Brass 100
Brigid 21
Brownies 73,78,88,90,112,123,127,128
Brown Man of the Muirs 88
Buff Meadow Cap 35
Buggane 103
Bwbachod 65

Cailleach Bheur 110
Cait Sith 113
Cabbyl Ushtey 102
Cedar 21
Changelings 12, 41,59, 63, 65
Chimbley Charlie 26
Christmas Day 5
Cleary Bridget 41
Cleary Michael 41
Clover 47

Clurican 95
Coblynau 10,62
Cocks 133
Colepexy Fingers 38
Colepexy 39
Collen 33
Coly Pixy 30
Col-Pixying 30
Conan Doyle 23
Connlas Well 56
Cream clot 35
Crowd 104
Cruithne 98
Cowslips 47
Cu Sith 113
Cwn Annwn 66
Cylchau Tylwyth Teg 67

Daniel O Donoghue 95
Daoine Sidhe 98
Daisies 47
Dead Hunt 93
Devils Dandy Dogs 12
Devils Tithe 41
Dog of Bouley 43
Dryads 125
Dublachan 97
Duergar 125
Dwarves 125

Each Uisge 112
Eilian of Garth Darwen 105
Elder 47,52,57
Ellyllon 62
Ellylldon 66
Elm 21
Elves 7,52,126

Fachan 132
Faerie Courts 35
Faerie Dances 35
Faerie Fetch 79
Faerie Hills 46,115
Faerie Hole 43
Faerie Islands 70
Faerie Lights 75
Faerie Market 30
Faeries Money 30
Faerie Plants 47
Faerie Rade 11,97
Faerie Rings 34, 35
Fairy Ring Champignon 35
Faerie Stones 38

INDEX

Faerie Walks 35
Faerie Wand 50
Faerie Well 30
Fair Family/ Fair Folk 62, 63
Farisees 45
Fear Dearc 99
Fear Garta 97
Fenodree 102
Feriers/Ferishers 45
Ferishey 102
Festivals 21
Fintan 56
Finvarra 97
Fir 21
Fir Darrig 96
Firbolgs 70,94,99
Flower Barrow Army 37
Formorians 70,94,99
Foxglove 47
Frid 130

Gabbygammies 38
Gallitrap 31
Gancener 99
Garlic 40
Garters 40
Gathornes 10
Gentry 96
Ghillie Dhu 130
Glashans 103
Glaistig 114
Glastonbury Thorn 32
Gnomes 60
Goblin 64,75,83,111,114,135
Goldenrod 48
Good Neighbours 110
Good People 93
Gowdie Isobel 125
Grace Hutchens 19
Green Lady of Caerphilly 63
Grey Neighbours 111
Griggs 29
Grugach 122
Gwarwyn a throt 65
Gwragedd Annwn 66
Gwyllion 62
Gwynn ap Nudd 33

Hag Stones 38
Hag Tracks 35
Hairy Meg 128
Halloween 5,21,30,67,100,121
Hawthorn 21,47, 56,132

Hazel 21,56, 82,132
Heartsease 56
Heather 48
Henkies 111
Herb Bennett 48
Hob 75,81
Hobbedys Lantern 79
Hobgoblins 81
Hogboy/Hogboon 129,130
Holly 48, 59,132
Hollyhocks 48
Holy Grail 32,
Holy Stones 38
Horseshoe 6,133
Hound of the Baskervilles 23,
Hounds 45,66
Howlaa Manx 104
Hunky Punk 28
Hutchens Rev John 38
Hyster Sprites 58

Imbolc 21, 59
Iron 5,6,100

Jack o Lantern 58
Jenny Burnt Tail 18
Jenny Greenteeth 81
Joan the Wad 18,
Joseph of Arimathea 32

Kelpie 39, 94,111,113,121
Kilmoulis 78
Kirk Robert 121
Kit with the Candlestick 121
Klippe 110
Knockers 10

Lady Day 5,
Lammas Tide 70
Lantern Man 58
Lavender 48
Lazy Lawrence 30,39
Leanhaun Shee 97
Leprechaun 21,92,96
Ley Lines 59,75
Lilac 48
Lil'Fellas 104
Loch Ness Monster 113
Lorntie 130
Lughnasadh 21,
Lunantishness 96
Lutey 15,

INDEX

Mab 62,99
Malekin 53
Manx Faeries 104
Manannan Mac Lir 102
Mathew Trewella 13,14,
Maunday Thursday 17,
May Day 5,18,
May Eve 34, 58
Maypole 21,
Meadow Puffball 35
Meppom James 45
Mermaids 12,13,14,15,23,37,67,68,6,72, 75,76,78,103,108,109,130,135
Merrows 93
Midsummer Day 5
Midsummer Eve 30,52,56,67
Milesians 94
Mob 104
Morgawr 13
Morgan 66
Morning Glory 48
Morra 17,
Muryan 10,

Nanny Diamonds 39
Nature Spirits 7
Nichiven 115
Nuadu 94
Nuckalavee 110
Nuggie 121
Nymphs 65,68,84

Oak 12,21,48, 57
Oak Men 26
Old People 10
Oonagh 97
Ozarks 7

Padfoot 78
Pansy 48
Passamaquaddy 7
Pechs/ Pehts 131
Peg O Nell 79
Peg Powler 81
Peggy wi' the Lantern 75
People Of Peace 93
Pharisees 45
Phynnodderee 104
Picts 98,131
Pisking 30
Pixyhunting 30
Pixieland 26

Pixies 10,12,17,19,20,24,26,30,31,52
Pixywarding 30
Plant Rhys Pwfen 63
Pooka 96
Portunes 11
Primroses 48,70
Puck 88
Puddlefoot 123
Punky Night 30

Redcap 131
Robin Goodfellow 88
Rowan 5,6,48,58,132
Roy Dog / Row Dog 37
Roy John 125

Samhain 21,30,33, 58
Satyr 84
Seahorse 19
Selkies 108
Scotch Bonnet 35
Shelley 123
Shoopi Hee 104
Shug Monkey 58
Sidhe 93,113
Silent Moving Folk 130
Skillywidden 12,
Sliochd Nan Ron 108
Sleigh Beggey 104
Sluagh 120
Small People 10,
Smugglers 15,
Spriggans 15,
Sprite 88
Spunkies 30
Spunky 29
St Georges Mushroom 35
St Johns Wort 48
Still Folk 110
St Patrick 56,99
Strangers 58,73

Tarans 110
Taroo Ushtey 102
Tash/Tershi 97
Tchi-co 43
Thomas the Rhymer 115,117,119,121
Thorn 12,48,96
Thyme 48
Tiddy Men /Tiddy Ones/ Tiddy People 58
Tir Nan'Og 93
Tom Trevarrow 10,

INDEX

To-tit tot 65
Trefeglwys 63
Trod 12
Trows 111,129
Trwtyn tratyn 65
Tuatha De Danann 94,95,99
Tylwyth Teg 63,67

Urisk 131

Veasta 38
Verry Volk 63

Walsh, John 37
Wag at the Wall 125
Walpurgis Night 21
Water Leaper 62
Wee Folk 110
White Hounds 33
White Lady of Wellow 29
Whooper of Sennen Cove 13
Wild Hunt 33
Wild Pansy 56
William Nay 19
Will o the Wisp 28,58, 66,79,121
Willy Wilcocks Hole 13
Witches 21,24,34,125
Wolf Pit Children 55
Woman of the Mist 29
Worm 26,110

Yallery Brown 58
Yarthkins 58
Yeth Hounds 12, 23
Yew 57
Yuletide 59
Ynnis Wtryn 32, 33